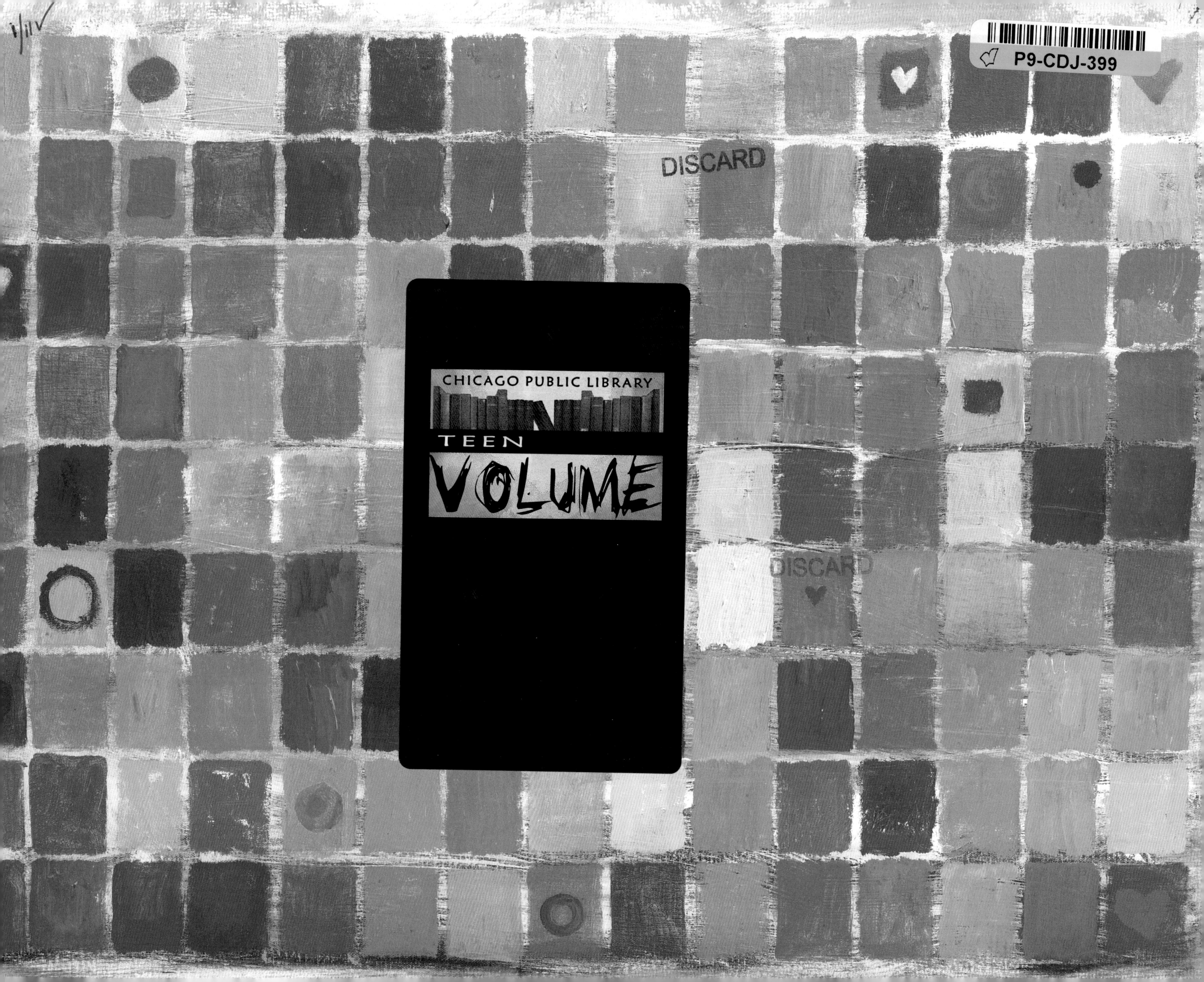

HEART TRANSPLANT

ANDREW
VACHSS

FRANK
CARUSO

ZAK MUCHA, LCSW

Book design by Jeff Schulz / Command-Z Design
Creative Production: Noelle Schloendorn

Published by Dark Horse Books
10956 SE Main Street
Milwaukie, Oregon 97222
darkhorse.com

Library of Congress Cataloging-in-Publication Data
Vachss, Andrew H. / Caruso, Frank T.
Heart Transplant / Andrew Vachss / Frank Caruso
ISBN 978-1-59582-575-9
1. Bullying. 2. Parenting. 3. Young Adult.
Printed by TWP Sdn Bhd, Malaysia
First Edition: October 2010
1 3 5 7 9 10 8 6 4 2

DARK HORSE BOOKS

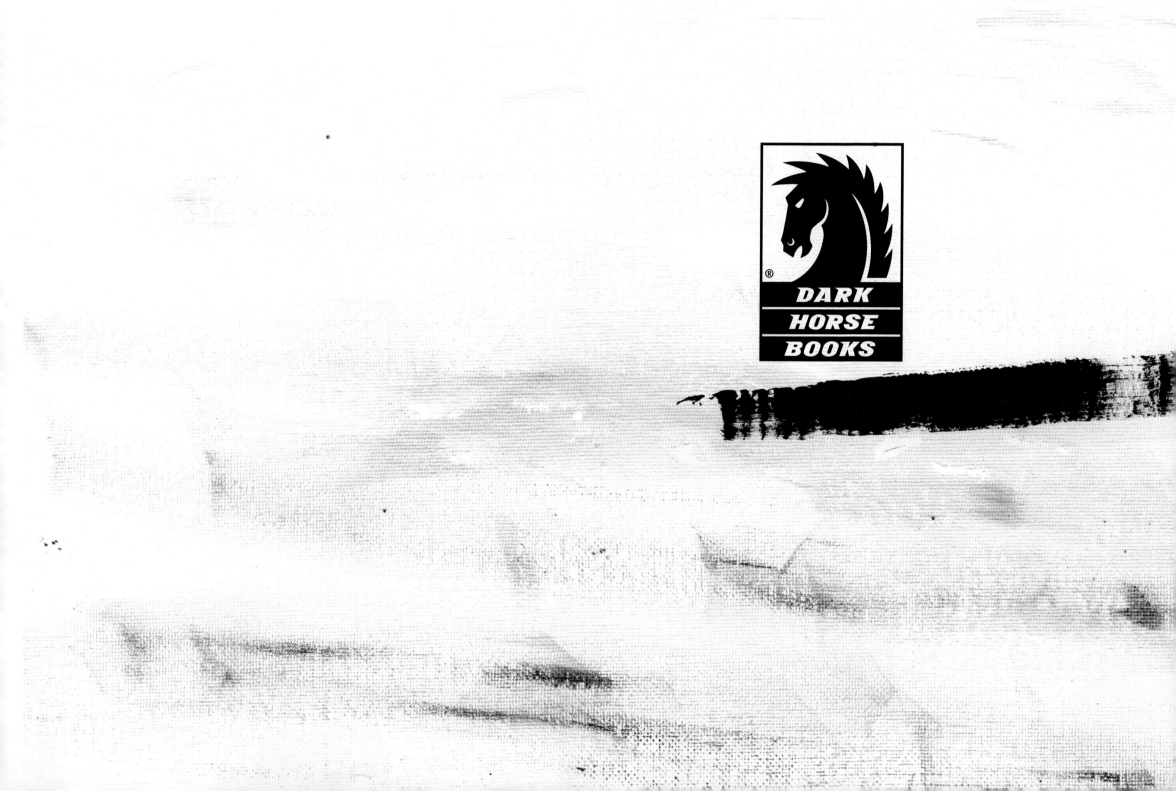

People love the movies. They worship them like they're some kind of god. But what good is a god you can't believe in?

I used to think about stuff like that all the time.

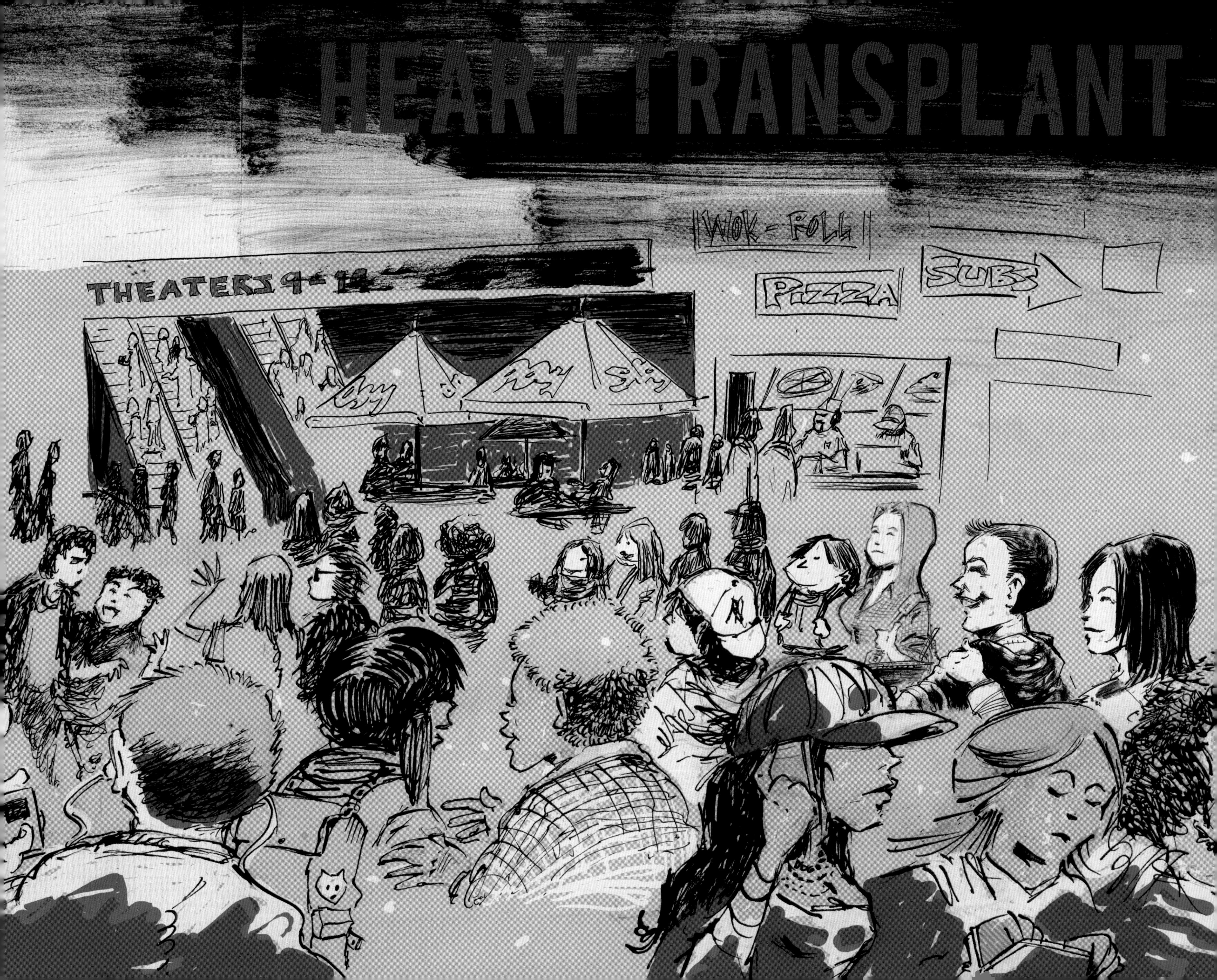
HEART TRANSPLANT
THEATERS 9-14
WOK-ROLL
PIZZA
SUBS

In the movies, cliques rule every school. They might be jocks; they might be thugs. They might just be pretty. Or rich, or whatever. But no matter what made them whatever they were, they always ran in packs. Even if one of those packs might look down on another one — like the way the stoners sneer at the jocks — there's one thing they all agree on: kids like me.

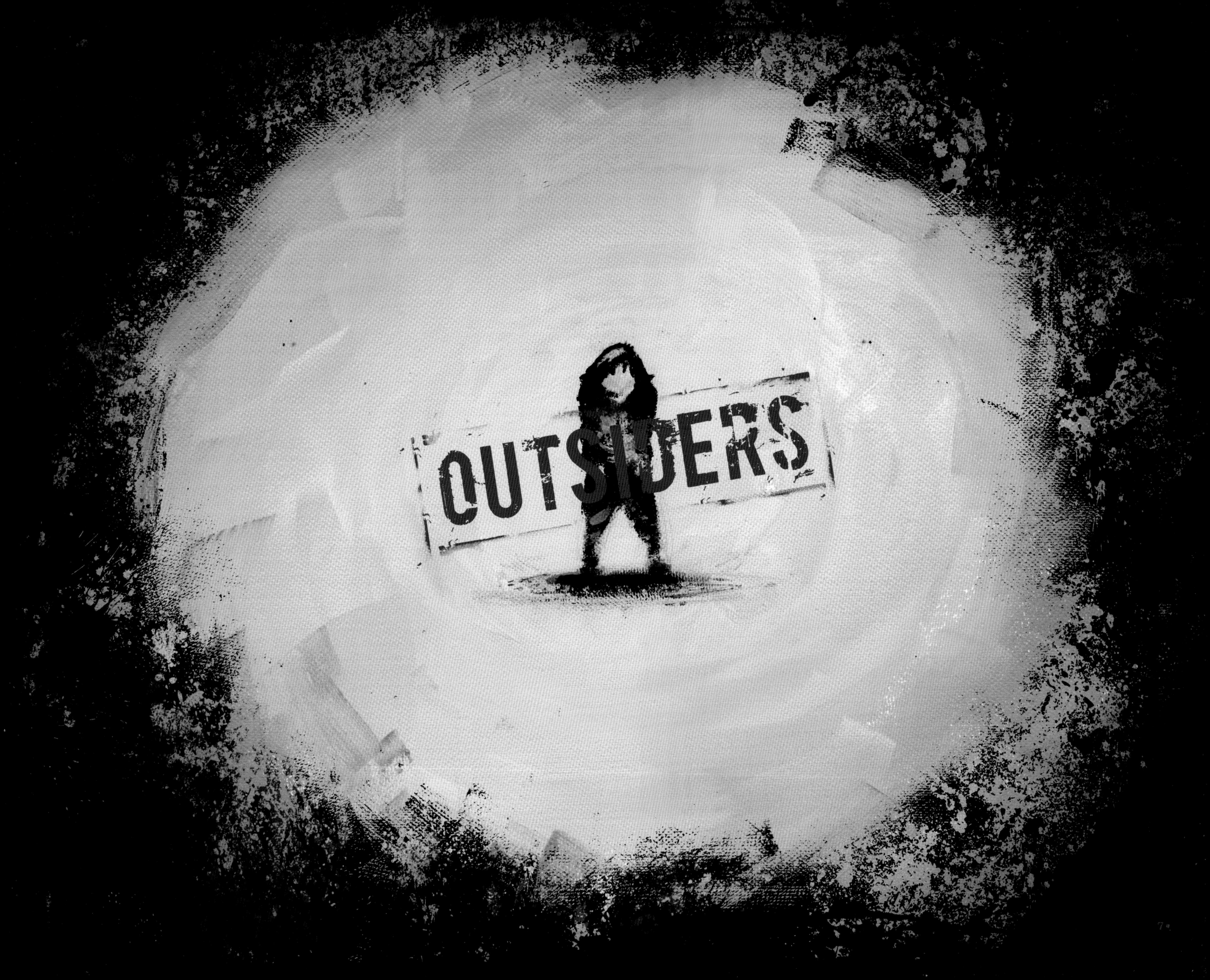
OUTSIDERS

An outsider could be a nerd, or a geek, or even one of those kids they call "special." All they had to be was different. Even being a fat kid qualified. Especially for the girls.

PHOTO
NOT
AVAILABLE

Most of the time, kids like that — kids like me — we were INVISIBLE. The only time anyone ever saw us was when they needed someone to make themselves look big. By making us small.

The movies always start off with that kind of truth.
But, just when they have you sucked in, it all turns into lies.

In the movies, the outsider kid always ends up with the beautiful girl at the end. Maybe he starts out following her around like a puppy, watching from a distance as she kisses her boyfriend. Then he ends up running errands for her, or doing her homework. Maybe he even pays her to go out with him, in some weird scheme to build a rep, so the other kids would think he was a new kind of cool, one they weren't hip to yet.

And the way it turns out — in the movies, I mean — the beautiful girl eventually sees what a wonderful person the outsider kid really is. What he is *inside*, I mean. Kind, sincere, faithful, loving. And everyone knows, *that* counts a lot more than good looks, or being a star athlete, or having a nice car.

Sure.

It works the same way for the outsider girls.
In the movies, I mean. They always end up with the
king of the school. Maybe one of the "players" takes a bet that he
can transform her from an ugly duckling into a hot chick, just to show he can
do it. But then he discovers the outsider girl was a goddess all along. All she has to do is
take off those glasses, get her hair done, put on some makeup, and *presto!* she's Megan Fox.

Or maybe the school makes the geeky girl tutor the star football player, so he can stay eligible
for the big game. Spending all that time together, they get to know each other. After a while,
none of that superficial stuff matters anymore.

Right.

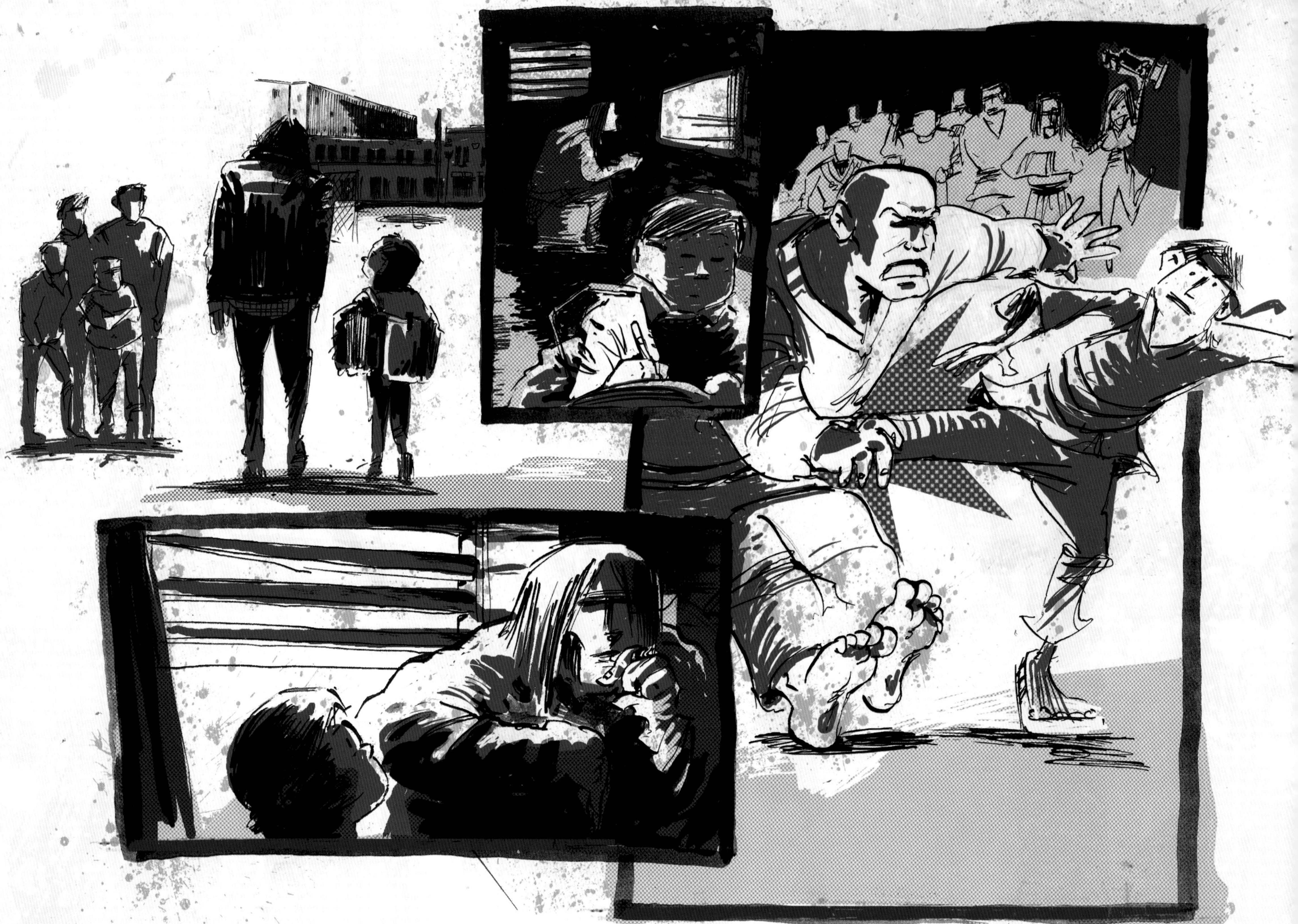

ESTABLISHING:

SERIES OF QUICK-CUTS: A MAN-SIZED YOUTH CAREFULLY PEERING OUT
THE WINDOW OF A BASEMENT TO SEE IF HE HAS ELUDED HIS PURSUERS,
A MUCH SMALLER KID IN THE FOREGROUND; THE SAME KID BEING
"SCHOOLED" BY THE OLDER, LARGER YOUTH, WATCHING WORSHIPFULLY AS
THE BIGGER KID SMOKES A CIGARETTE; THAT SAME RUNT FACING A MENACING
GROUP WITH A SCHOOL -- WHICH LOOKS MORE LIKE A FACTORY -- LOOMING
IN THE BACKGROUND, BUT THE RUNT IS STANDING NEXT TO THE MUCH
LARGER, SELF-ASSURED YOUTH HE HAD ALLOWED TO HIDE IN HIS BASEMENT;
THE RUNT, THIS TIME A FEW YEARS OLDER, DELIVERING A MIGHTY KARATE KICK
TO AN OPPONENT'S MID-SECTION AS A CROWD CHEERS IN THE BACKGROUND....

[POV CLEARLY INDICATES THAT THESE ARE "MIND PICTURES," AS THE
SPEAKER IS NEVER ON-SCREEN.]

SEAN
(V/O: PURE INTERIOR MONOLOGUE)

In the movies, the kid who gets picked on by every
bully in the school makes pals with some real tough
kid. Maybe he starts off by paying him, like a
bodyguard. Or maybe he finds out that he's really
not a stupid thug, he's only got dyslexia. The
outsider kid shows him how to get help for that,
and they're pals for life.

Or they can make it happen from the other direction.
One night, the tough guy needs a place to hide -- the
cops are after him for something. The outsider kid
lets him hide in the basement of his house. He does
that because he thinks they're friends ... and he
never tells. That's when the tough guy discovers the
outsider kid really <u>is</u> his friend. And nobody better
try and push his friend around!

If all else fails, they can always write it so some
old guy teaches the weak kid karate. A few weeks later,
the kid takes the top prize in some tournament and
wins everyone's respect.

He gets the girl too, of course.

Always the same: before the movie ends, the outsider
kid isn't an outsider anymore.

In real life, the kids all wear uniforms.

The JOCKS PARADE AROUND IN THEIR VARSITY JACKETS,

The TOUGH GUYS WEAR DENIM SHIRTS,.. BUTTONED TO THE THROAT.

The GOTHS.

The BOARDERS,

EVEN The CHEERLEADERS.

The GARAGE BANDS.

The PRINCESSES

They all flash their brands.
Like it was some kind of medal they'd earned.

It doesn't matter how the movie starts off,
something always happens to teach the kids
that brand names don't mean a thing.

What's an Escalade with twenty-two-inch rims compared to a
hydrogen-powered transport module some teenage genius built
in his own garage? How can gold chains and FUBU gear compete
with a true and honest heart?

Movies always tell a story.
And it's always a lie.

Mom said I had to call Brian "Daddy." She always made me do that, every time a new man came to live with us.

The only thing Brian ever tried to teach me was how to break into houses. "Even if you get caught, so what? You're a little kid; they can't put you in jail or anything. You go into this room, they yell a bunch of bull at you, pound on the desk a few times ... then they just let you go home with your mother."

We were standing behind the backyards of some houses that night. One looked like nobody was home. It probably was as easy as Brian said it would be. But I wouldn't do it. Not because it was wrong or anything. All I remember for sure was how much I hated Brian.

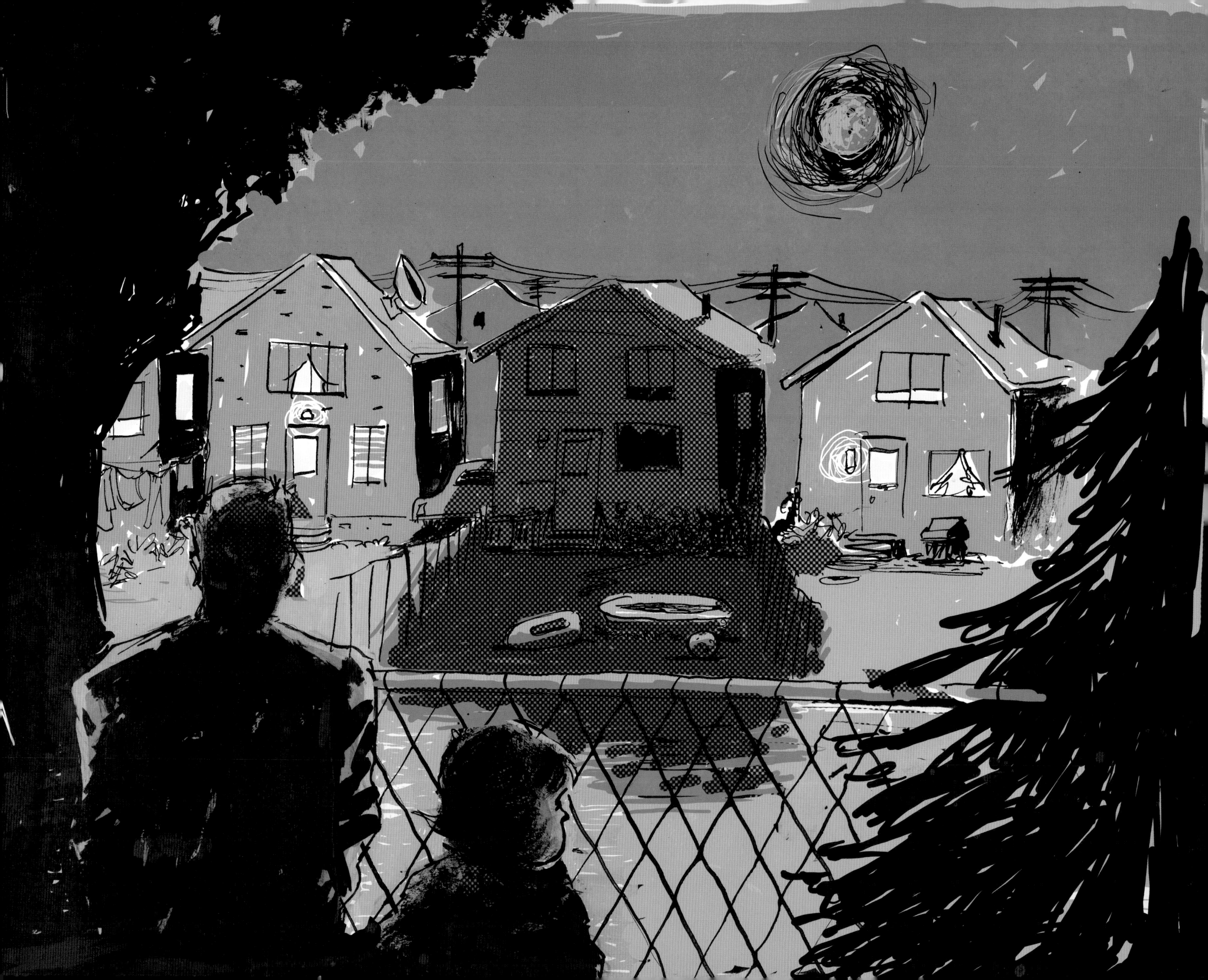

Brian told me I was a useless little nothing. I'd never be a real man, like him. "You're probably already a fairy-boy," he spit at me. "You wouldn't last an hour in jail. Get outta my sight, punk. Go home and cry to your momma."

I did go home, but I didn't cry to my mother. I knew better than that.

Brian came back a few hours later. He woke me up and punched me around for a while, calling me a fat little punk and all kinds of dirty names while he was doing it.

My mother kept on watching TV.
I didn't cry then, either. Brian's fists really hurt, but when I saw he'd come back without any loot, I knew he was a bigger coward than I'd ever be.

Those sappy movies are usually PG-13, but they're not for kids; they're for grownups who want to believe life always turns out right. Kids want the real thing — you know, like a maniac with a machete who hunts pretty girls in bikinis.

THE SUMMER CAMP SLASHER

It's supposed to be funny when a scrawny little kid gets stuffed into a locker. Or when they give him a wedgie, or toilet-face him. Those kids are never really terrified, just ... resigned. That's their role, and they play it.

Later, when they reminisce about their school days, they'll even laugh about it.

But that's another lie.

The truth is, some of those kids will do just
about anything, always trying to find a way to fit in.
But the only place they ever fit is into their lockers.
Or on their knees, in a basement where there was
supposed to be a "party" they'd put on their best dress for.

The movies all have the same message: **All you need is patience and hard work.** It always comes out right, even if it takes a few years.

Just keep watching and you'll see how the nerd makes a gazillion bucks, and comes back to the school's ten-year reunion behind the wheel of a Ferrari. All the guys who used to bully him, *they're* the nothings now. Fat and bald and pumping gas for a living. Now they all line up to admire the nerd's fancy stuff. And that beauty queen is all over him.

There's a thousand versions of that ending, but one thing you can count on: virtue always triumphs, and bullies always get what's coming to them.

Karma, you know?

What goes around ...

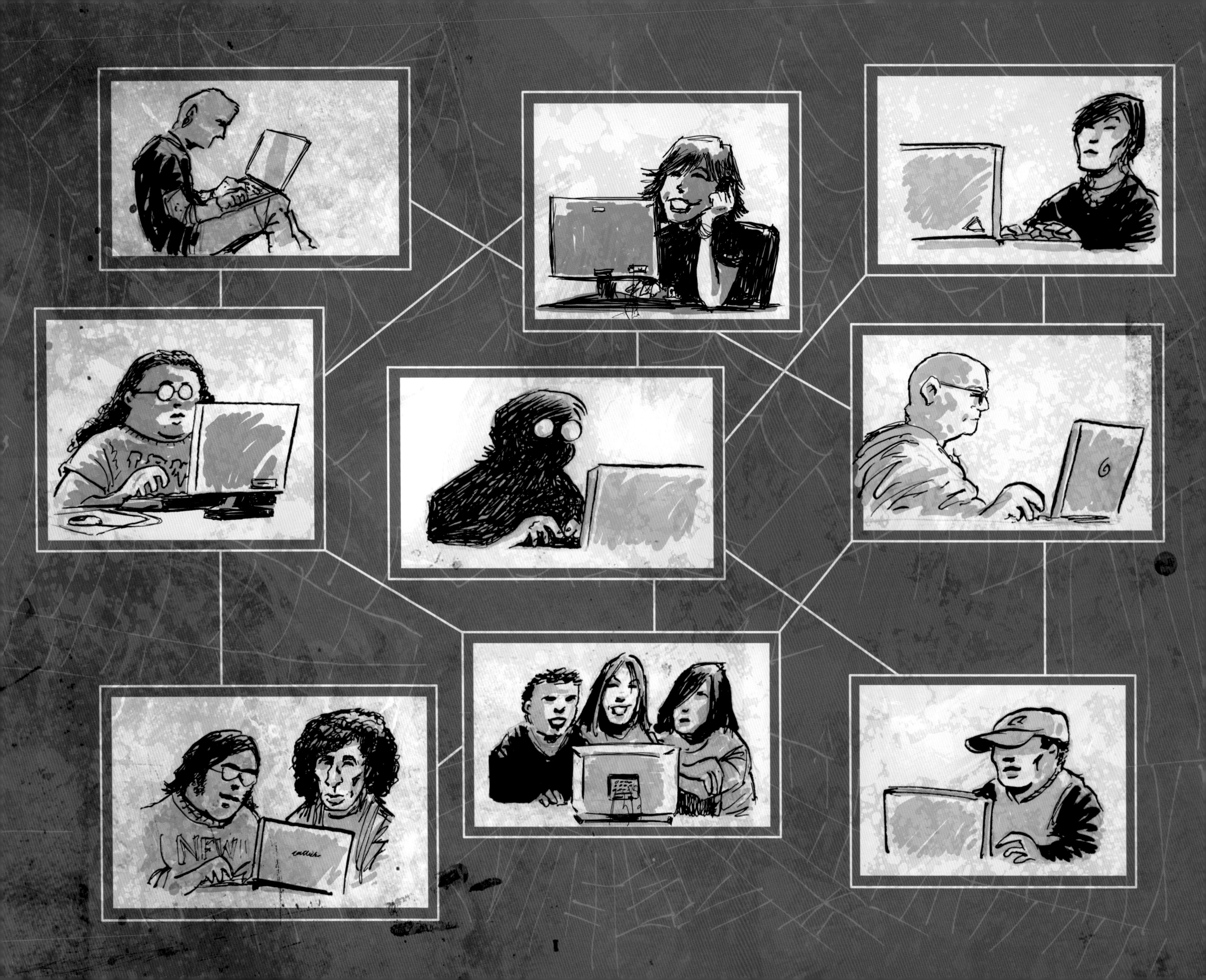

Maybe I had never learned how to break into houses, but I learned how to break into other things. I taught myself.

At first, I did it because I thought I'd finally found a club that would let me join. Even *wanted* me. Hackers are just like kids at school; they break down into groups, and they only run with their own kind. There's black hats and white hats, pranksters and vandals, code-writers and exploiters ... all kinds of different ones.

There's lots of places where you can make friends with other people. The great thing is that, when you're online, nobody knows who you are. Who you *really* are, I mean.

Sometimes, that's not such a great thing. Sometimes, your "friends" are people who want to hurt other people, just for fun — the way bullies do.

I could stop being an outsider, but that was only when I was inside a world that wasn't real. And that world isn't safe, no matter what some people think.

So I went back to being myself. Being *by* myself.

But I didn't give up. I kept studying, searching for a way. All my teachers said I was smart; I knew I could find an answer, somewhere.

"CYBER-PRANK" DRIVES TEEN TO SUICIDE

blue mary's blog

Nobody will ever love me.
And nobody will miss me
when I'm gone.

OFFICIALS IGNORED CYBER WARNINGS

DIARY OF HATE > MY PERSONAL HIT LIST

I HATE THEM. I HATE THEM ALL.
ONE DAY, REAL SOON
THEY'LL SEE HOW MUCH I HATE THEM.
THEN THE WHOLE WORLD WILL KNOW.

CYBER-STALKING CALLED "SERIOUS THREAT TO NATION'S YOUTH"

She's always looking at me in class.
I know what she's thinking.
I hope she's reading this.
She knows who I'm thinking about.
And I *know* she knows.

Posted by NinjaRapeTorture at 3:50 a.m.

One time, I asked my grandfather to watch one of those movies with me. Not because I thought he'd like the movie — he always said any movie made after the Fifties was pansy tripe — but because I thought he might be able to explain something to me.

There was nobody else to ask. There's just me and him, and he wasn't even really my grandfather.

The reason I lived with him was that my mother and Brian were killed. Shot to death while I was at school. I came home and found them — two more wrecked things in a wrecked apartment. The cops said nobody had heard the shots, nobody had seen anything.

It was like Nobody came in there and killed them.

The Welfare lady was there, too. She said they would have to put me in "placement" until they found a suitable foster home. I figured they said "placement" because they really meant some kind of jail for kids.

The only thing the cops asked me was where I had been before I called 911. I could tell they had already checked. I'd only come back early that day because it was so bitter cold outside.

Usually, I would wait until it was getting late. Maybe Brian would already be out. That would be better — my mother would be too busy crying about Brian cheating on her to care about hitting me.

The cops took off. All I remember was hearing one of them say something about "half a dozen keys" ... but he was talking to another cop when he said that, not to me.

Then this big man just opened the door and walked in. He acted like he'd been there a hundred times, but I'd never seen him before.

He told the Welfare lady he was the father of the man my mother had been living with. **"That's his kid, there, yeah? So I guess he's my responsibility now."**

The Welfare lady didn't pay much attention; she was busy making a thousand phone calls. The old man pulled me off into the bedroom. The apartment only had the one; I slept wherever I could. There was a couch in the living room, in front of the TV, but at least one of them was always on it.

"I know you're just about out of
choices, boy," he said. Real soft,
so nobody else could hear. "Just
about out of time to make them, too.
Nine years old, no court's gonna
let you live on your own; they're gonna
send you someplace. But you tell them
I'm your grandfather, they'll be happy
to dump you on me. 'Specially 'cause it
won't cost 'em nothing."

"But my real father—"

"You never had no real father," the old
man told me. His voice was hard as
steel, not fake-tough like the way
gangsters talked in the movies.
"When you say that word, 'father,'
you're only talking about the man
who got your mother pregnant.
And you've never even met
whoever that was, have you?"

I just sat there. A pudgy little kid.

I wasn't crying — I'd already learned never to do that.

But I nodded, confessing what I always thought was my deepest secret.

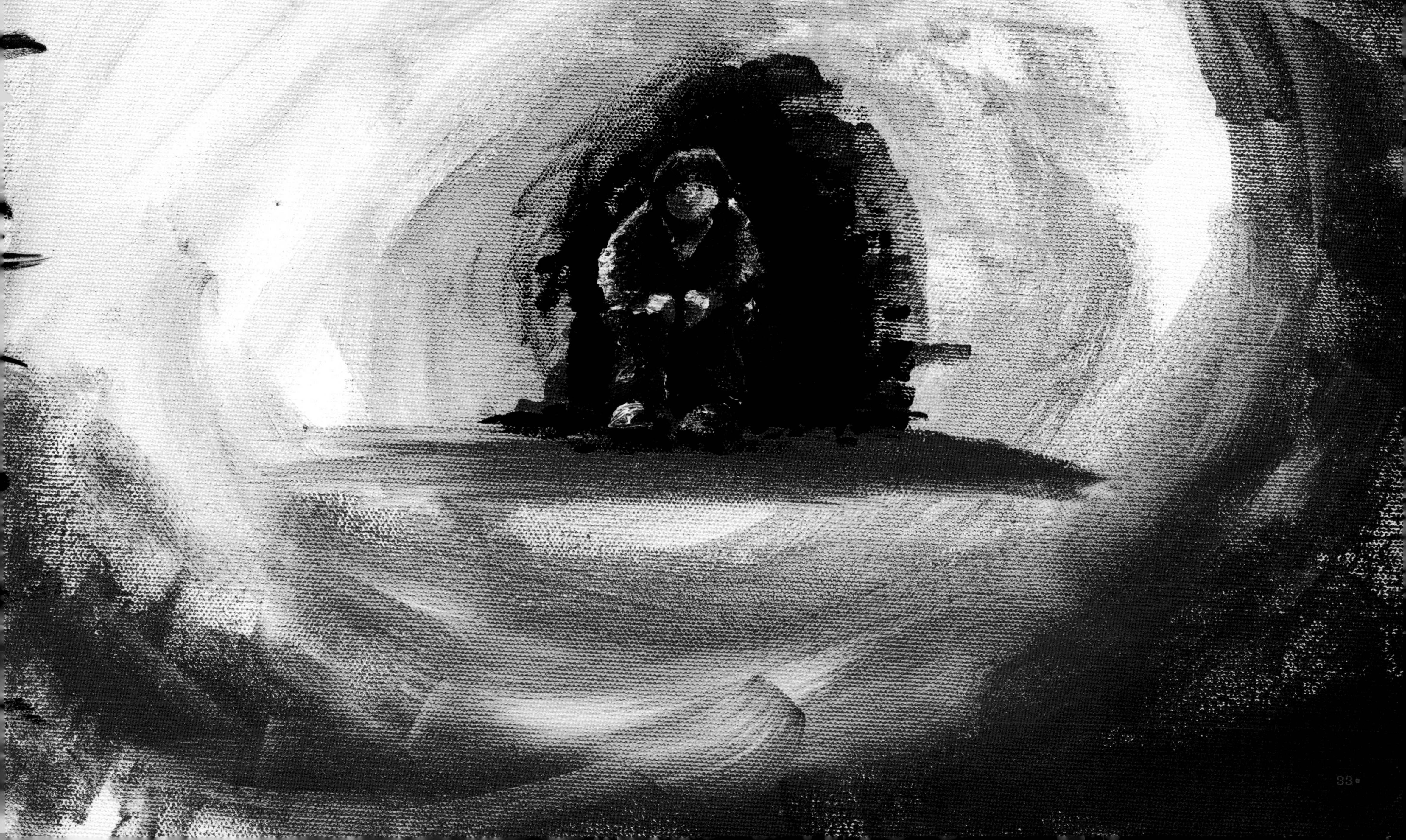

That "real father" I always dreamed of, he was a movie, too — a movie I made up inside my head. In that one, my real father never even knew I was alive. Then, one day, he learned about me by accident. I won some kind of award, and he saw my picture in the paper. That's when he came and took me away from my life. He was so proud. And he promised he'd make it all up to me, all those years.

"I don't owe that miserable sack of garbage nothing," the old man told me. "I'm not saying I was any great shakes at being his Da. But his mother, she was a saint too good for heaven. Treated the boy like he was made of glass-and-gold.

"School says he's suspended again, Maggie'd go right down there and fight with them. And when the miserable punk finally quits — that was his specialty, quitting — he never even thinks about working for a living. Not that one.

"He was a big, strong lad. Could have done a bunch of things, education or no. I coulda gotten him a union card, easy. He never even tried. I know his mother would sneak him money every time he came crawling around, but even that wasn't enough.

"Finally, we had to take out a new mortgage on the house to make his bail, and then hire some weasel of a lawyer just to keep him out of prison. Me, I would have let him rot in that jail until he had a trial, but Brian got his mother on the phone, crying like a little baby, and that was it. I couldn't say no to my Maggie, but having to ask me to start all over — we'd paid off the house only the year before — that was what finally made her heart give out.

"See, Brian was her only child. She wanted more — a whole houseful, she used to say — but the docs told her she couldn't. So Brian got all the love that was meant for a dozen.

"The filthy little swine called himself a man, but he lived off of women. And that killed the only woman who ever really loved him. Well, he picked his own life. Probably was taking most of your mother's Welfare check, like he always does."

I nodded again. What I didn't say was that Brian hadn't been the first man to do that.

"Sorry little sod finally saw his chance to make himself a big shot, I guess. Fancied himself a hard man, but he was soft as custard inside. Yellow as an egg yolk, he was, too.

"Me, I spit on him. It was him who put my Maggie in the ground, and he never even came to her funeral.

"But Maggie didn't go out alone, no.
I tell you, the hall wasn't big enough to
hold everyone who came to see her off.
Brian, they can pine-box that mangy
cur for all I give a damn — he's going
straight into the fire anyway."

I didn't know how the old man knew about the Welfare check. My mother had been so happy with Brian. She was a fat, sloppy drunk who found herself a younger, good-looking guy. Nothing else mattered to her. Nothing ever had.

"And my son, that corpse back there, he wasn't no kind of father, either," the old man said. It didn't feel like a question, but I couldn't figure out how he could have known how much I hated the man my mother made me call "Daddy."

"I got nothing so great to offer you,"
the old man whispered to me. **"Just a little house.
Nothing fancy, but not a puke-pit like this rathole.
The neighborhood's pretty rough, and getting rougher,
but it's a lot cleaner than this one, that's for sure.
I'll take care of you best I can, is all I can say."**

It was the best offer I'd ever had.

Pop — that's what I started calling him
after a while; he said it would make it
easier with the school — had a little brick
cottage in Queens, almost in the shadow
of the bridge to Manhattan.

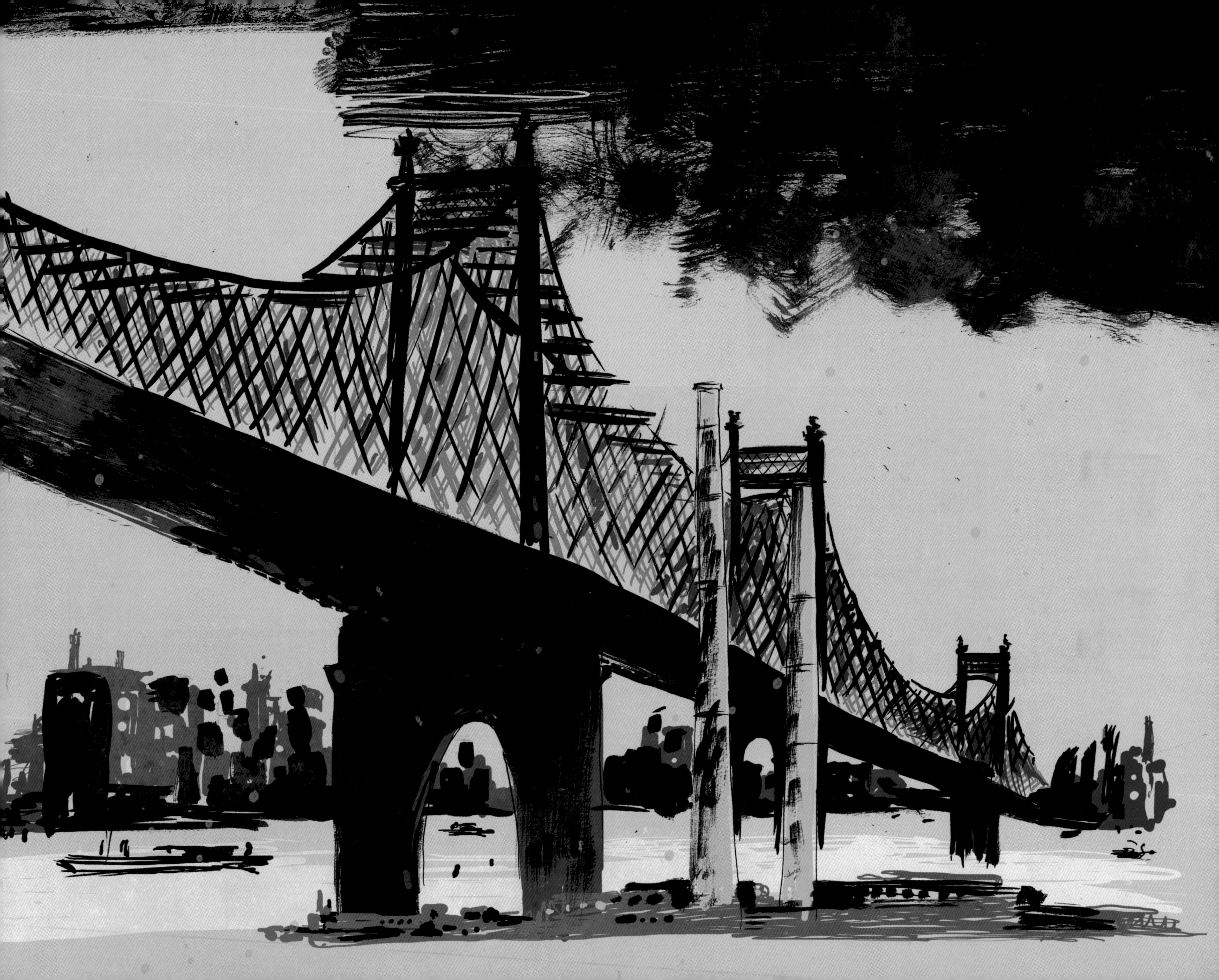

I had my own room! Even my own bathroom. Pop told me he was a lousy cook, but everything he made was a million times better than the take-out Mom and Brian lived on. And I could always have as much as I wanted.

Pop didn't have an Internet connection, but when I told him how we could get one right through the cable TV company, he said to find out what it would cost. After I told him, he went ahead and ordered it.

It was just like one of those movies really coming true.

My first Christmas with Pop, he gave me a beautiful new laptop. It was exactly what I wanted. Pop hadn't guessed that, he'd just asked me straight out. I'll never forget how that happened.

"Giving a man a present he don't want, that's a holy mess for all concerned," he told me. "The guy who gets it, he has to show appreciation, doesn't he? Pretend he loves the damn thing, whatever it is. But, inside, he really resents it, see? He figures, if his pal really knew him all that good, he'd know he wouldn't want whatever piece of crap came in that Christmas wrapping, got me?"

"Yes, sir," I said.

"You're a real good kid, Sean," he said. "And sharp as a fresh-stropped razor, too."

"What do you want for Christmas?" I said.

He gave me a look. "Me? I don't want—"

"Me, neither, then," I told him.

Pop lit a cigarette, watching me through the smoke like he does, sometimes.

I didn't move.

"You got real bulldog in you, boy," he finally said. Then he smiled. "Okay, I know when I'm beat. What I want is a good winter coat. I used to be able to work iron in the middle of January with nothing but a flannel shirt under that cable sweater my Maggie had knitted for me. But those days are long gone."

had been with Pop almost the whole year. So, by then, I knew what he meant. His idea of a good winter coat would be something that got the job done — he couldn't care less about brand names.

But I had asked him, so it was on me. Whatever a good winter coat cost, I'd have to get the money for it myself.

"The only way you find out if the other guy's bluffing is to call his hand," Pop always told me.

And I always listened to everything he ever said. Every single word. Because when my Pop spoke, he wasn't just talking: he was talking to *me*.

SALE

I found just the coat I was looking for. It was on sale, too. Kind of like a Navy pea coat,

but it had a hood and a couple of pouchy pockets, plus a flap that snapped shut over the zipper.

The coat was just hanging there by itself, like the flashy ones wouldn't let it hang with them.

One eighty-nine ninety-five. I added the tax in my head; a couple of bucks over two hundred, it would come to.

I left the coat behind. I knew it would still be there if I ever came back. Nobody'd want an old-style thing like that.

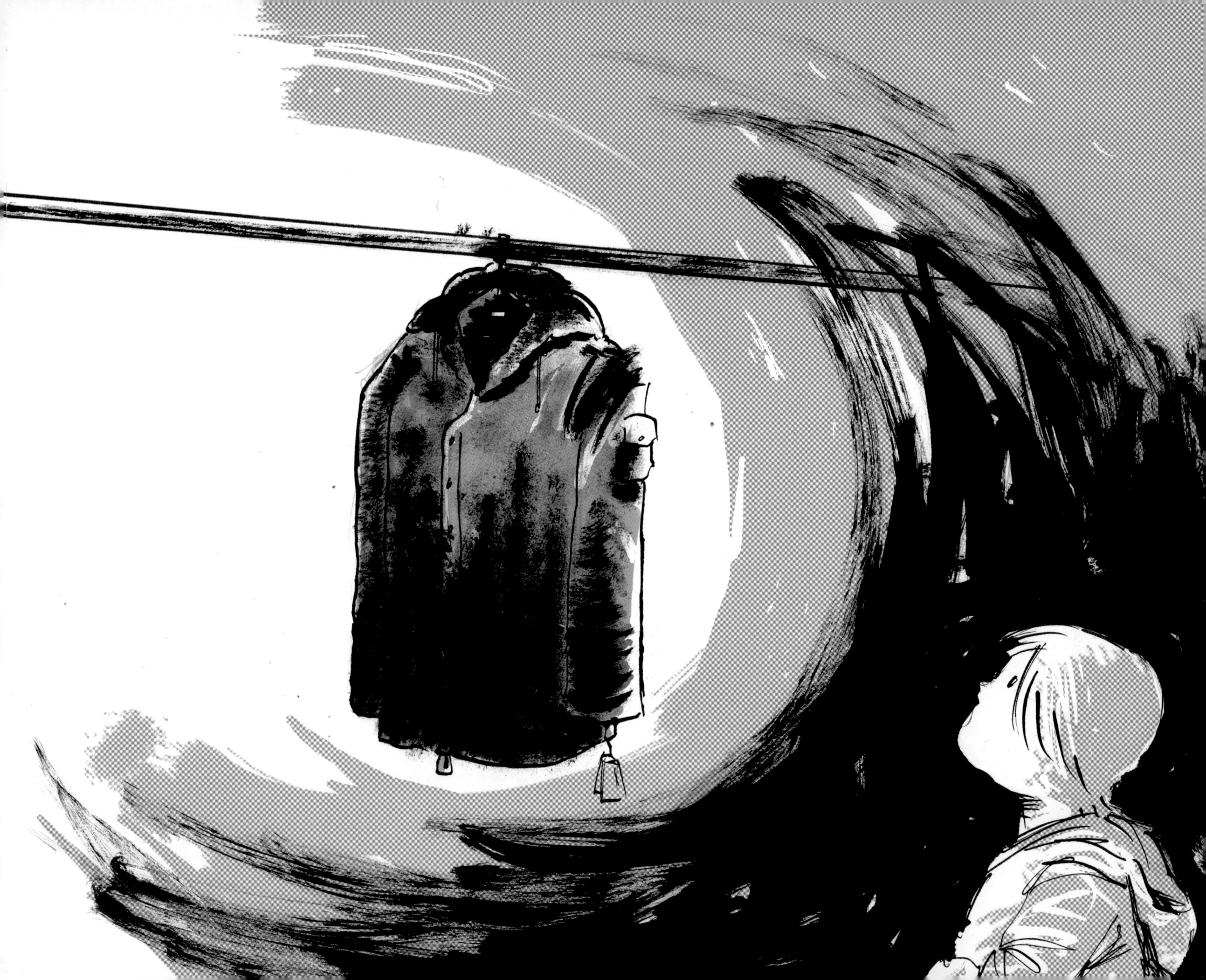

The store where I'd found the coat was part of a big chain. They had a Web site, where you could order their stuff online. And they had the exact same coat I wanted, only *there* it was two forty-nine plus delivery. That made it over thirty percent more than the one in the store. What a bunch of crooks.

Of course, you needed a credit card to order online. But that was no problem; I already had one. I'd memorized the number last summer, when a man in the fancy coffee place used it to pay for his double mocha grande. It went right into my notebook.

The next day, I went into the city and rented a mailbox in one of those little places you see all over. The Post Office won't take FedEx or UPS or anything like that. Plus, you need ID to rent a PO box. The place I found, all they wanted was the money.

I told the guy behind the counter that I was opening the box for my father. I never looked at him close, but I could see he was wearing a turban. He just said, "Fill out card." I gave him twelve dollars for the first month.

After that, I sent them a money order every month. I made sure to send mail to that box, too — I wanted them to get used to seeing me every few weeks.

Robert Louis Henderson II used his Visa card to buy the coat online. He requested the complimentary card the company would enclose if you filled out their form. He typed in: "Looks like the ones we wore back

in college, huh, Tommy? Merry Xmas, pal!" He also asked that the coat be gift-wrapped, and even paid extra for next-day delivery.

I knew the credit card was still good. Just like I knew that guy's home address, date of birth, Social Security number, even his bank account balance. I don't know what he did for a living, but he was very sloppy with his laptop, leaving the Wi-Fi connection open while he flirted with the girl behind the coffee counter.

I used one of the computers in the big public library to place the order.

Two days later, I went back into the city. There was a yellow slip in the box.

"Package," is all the man in the turban said when I showed it to him.

"Could I have it, please?"

"It is five dollars for package. We have to sign for Federal Express, so there is a charge."

Another thief. I gave him the money and took my package home.

I wasn't ever coming back. And if anyone ever asked who had rented that box, the guy would tell them about some fat white kid with big glasses ... if he remembered me at all.

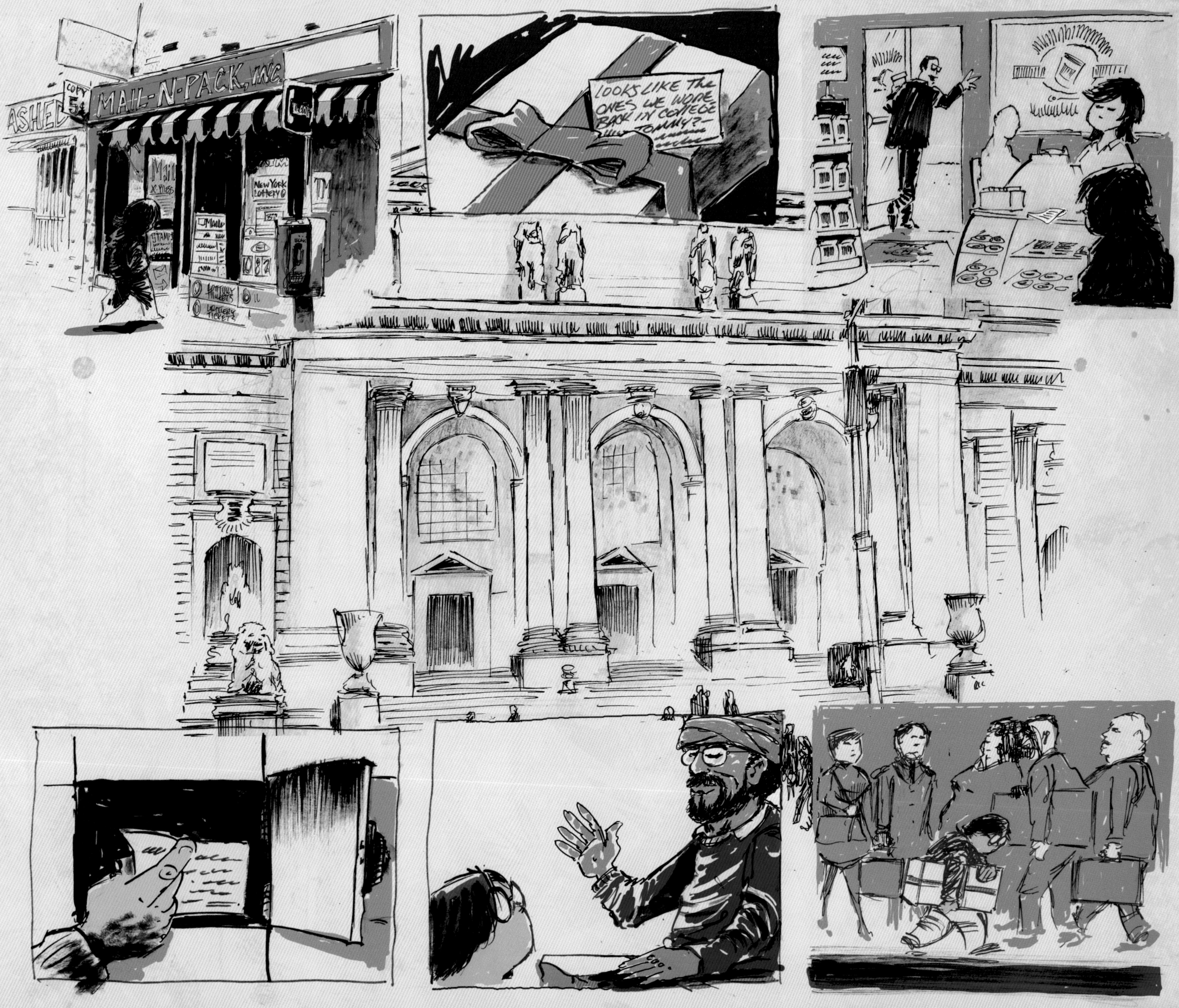

ASHED
COPY 5¢
MAIL-N-PACK, INC.
Mail X-PRESS
STAMPS
NEW YORK LOTTERY
LOTTERY TICKETS
LOOKS LIKE THE ONES WE WORE BACK IN COLLEGE TOMMY?—

See, we all look alike, fat kids. And I don't even wear glasses, so I was more invisible than usual. Still, I'd checked out a dozen of those mailbox places before I found one that didn't have security cameras.

Hiding the coat was easy. Pop never went in my room. I was responsible for keeping it clean, and he said I did a better job of that than he ever had.

I don't know if that was true because I never went in his room, either. A man is entitled to his privacy. Pop explained that part to me the day I asked him why he had knocked on the door to my room instead of just walking in.

But that didn't mean he wouldn't ask me questions.

"How'd you get named 'Sean'?"

"I don't know. It's what they always called me."

"How come you spell it 'Shawn'?"

"That's the way they said, when I started school."

"That's not the right way to spell your name, boy. You spell it 'Sean.' That's Irish."

By then, I knew I could ask *him* questions, too. So I said: "Am I Irish?"

"What do you call me?" he answered my question with one of his own — he was always doing that.

"Pop," I said, proud to be hearing myself saying that word.

"Okay, then. Now, if I'm Irish — which I sure to damn-the-Brits am — what's that make you?"

"Irish?"

"You get straight A's on your report cards, and you couldn't have figured that one out for yourself, son?"

It was the first time anyone ever called me that.

Pop loved his winter coat. **"Ah, it's bloody gorgeous!"** he said, hefting it in his big hands. **"If I had my choice of all the coats in the world, this would have been the very one I'd've picked for myself. I'll bet there's none so fine anywhere."**

He was still raving about the coat when he suddenly looked over at me.

"What're you crying about, boy? I told you, I—"

"I ... I'm just happy."

"Damn, Sean. If that don't prove you're Irish, the Pope's a flaming Orangeman!"

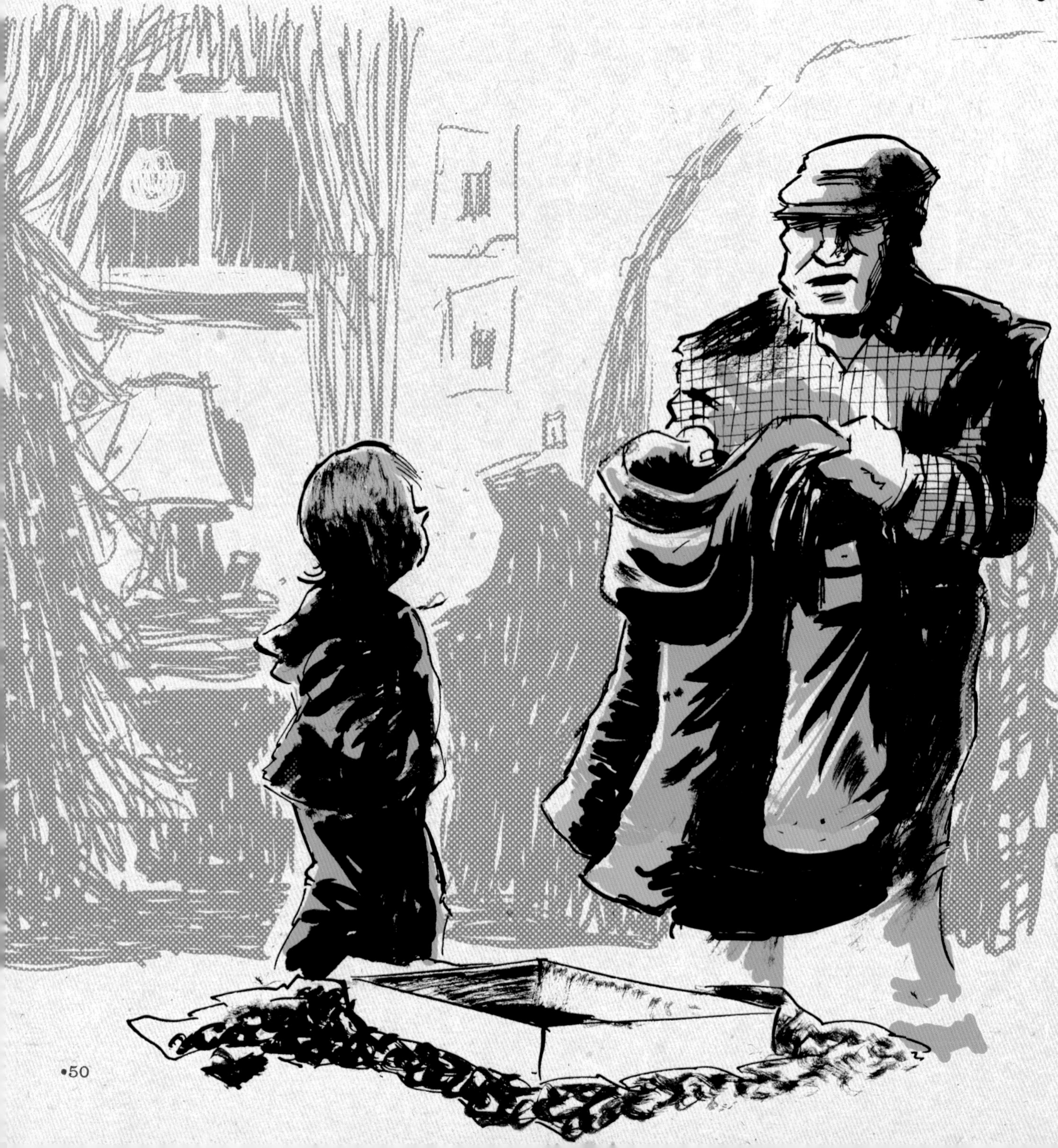

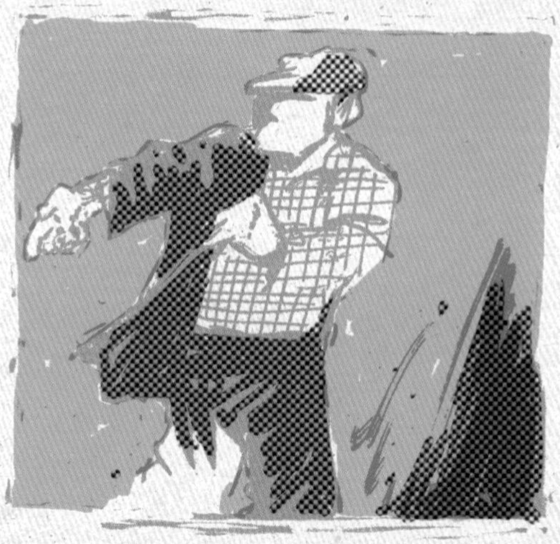

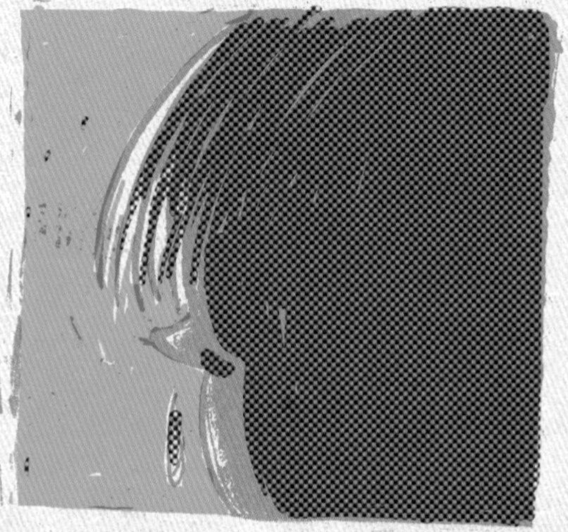

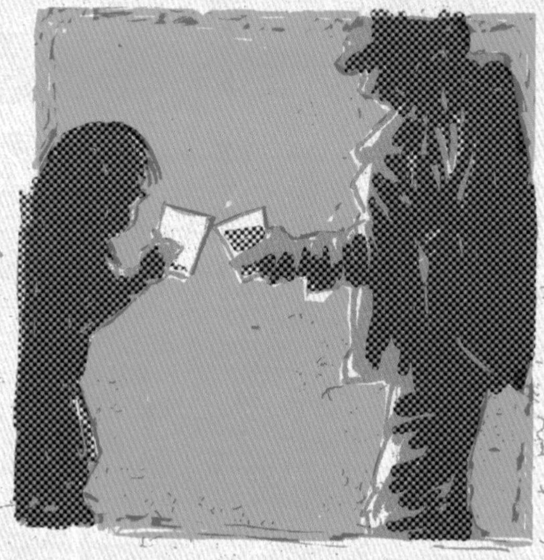

I had my first taste of whiskey that night. Just a couple of drops, really. I didn't much like it, but, sitting there with Pop, battery acid would have tasted like sweet honey in my mouth.

It was all just lovely — that's what Pop called stuff that he really liked — until I got to junior high.

That's when things really started happening to me.

Every day, the same things.

Some worse than others. But all bad, all the time.

Girls being around, sometimes even watching,
that made it worse than ever.
I wasn't sure why, but I know it did.

I don't know why they all acted like it was so funny.
I mean, girl cliques bullied other girls, too. Nasty, mean, vicious...
You would see the girls they hurt trying not to show it, but I knew.
Still, every time it happened to me, even *those* girls laughed with the others.

"What in holy hell happened to you, boy?"

I told Pop I fell down the stairs at school.

He gave me a look, but he didn't say anything more.

A man is entitled to his privacy.

ut he kept asking.
So, one day, I finally
told him. "It didn't
hurt me," I said.

"Yeah, it did."

"It didn't, Pop.
I didn't cry or—"

**"I'm not talking about
you taking a beating, son.
No man goes through life
without catching a few of
those. But a beating ain't the
same thing as being made dirt
of. Being humiliated. So don't
be telling me it didn't hurt you,
'cause it hurts me. Inside me,
it hurts. So I know it hurts
you, too. I even know where
it hurts."**

"I would never hurt you,
Pop."

**"I know you wouldn't, Sean.
Not for the world. But I know
what your plan is. And it's
no good."**

"My plan?"

"That's right, boy, your plan. I know you.
I know you always got a plan for everything.
I can see right inside your head. You're figuring,
now that you know it hurts *me* to see you all beat
up, all you got to do is make sure you keep them
from marking up your face. Just cover your face,
let 'em pound away on your body. I wouldn't be
able to see nothing then, would I?"

I sat there for a minute, trying to puzzle it
out. But I couldn't, so I just asked him.

"How can you do that?"

"Do what?"

"See inside my head."

"Ah, I can't see inside your head, son.
That's just an expression. But I can *feel* you,
right in here," he said, patting his chest.
"You and me, we got the same heart.
When your heart hurts, my heart feels that, too.
You understand that?"

"I ... think so."

"Well, you might think on *that* tonight.
Instead of your homework, for just this once."

"I will," I said.

In our house, "said" was the same as
"promised." Pop taught me that. When a
man says he's going to do something,
that's always a promise. I wasn't a man
yet, but Pop always said you had to get
ready to do something before you did it,
if you wanted to do it right. **"That's the
Irish curse, son. Jumping right in, I'm talking
about. I know you've heard me say that
over and over. That's how come you
turned into such a planner."**

He slapped himself lightly on the cheek, like he does when he suddenly remembers something.

"Damn me, I should have thought of this before. Listen, son: can you come by the Chieftain tonight? My old pal Conny's been taken home, and we'll all be going over there after the wake. I might have a bit of a bag on, and I don't want to walk home staggering down the street like some old drunk, not with those lace-curtain neighbors of ours. You come along and fetch your old Da around ten, will you? Just in case."

It was a few minutes before ten when I turned the corner that night and saw Pop standing outside the tavern.

He was kind of slouched against the wall, fumbling with his hands. I could see he was trying to light a cigarette, but he wasn't having any luck. Then I saw a flash of flame....

All of a sudden, three men ran up and jumped on him.

They knocked him down to the sidewalk.
They were kicking him and everything.

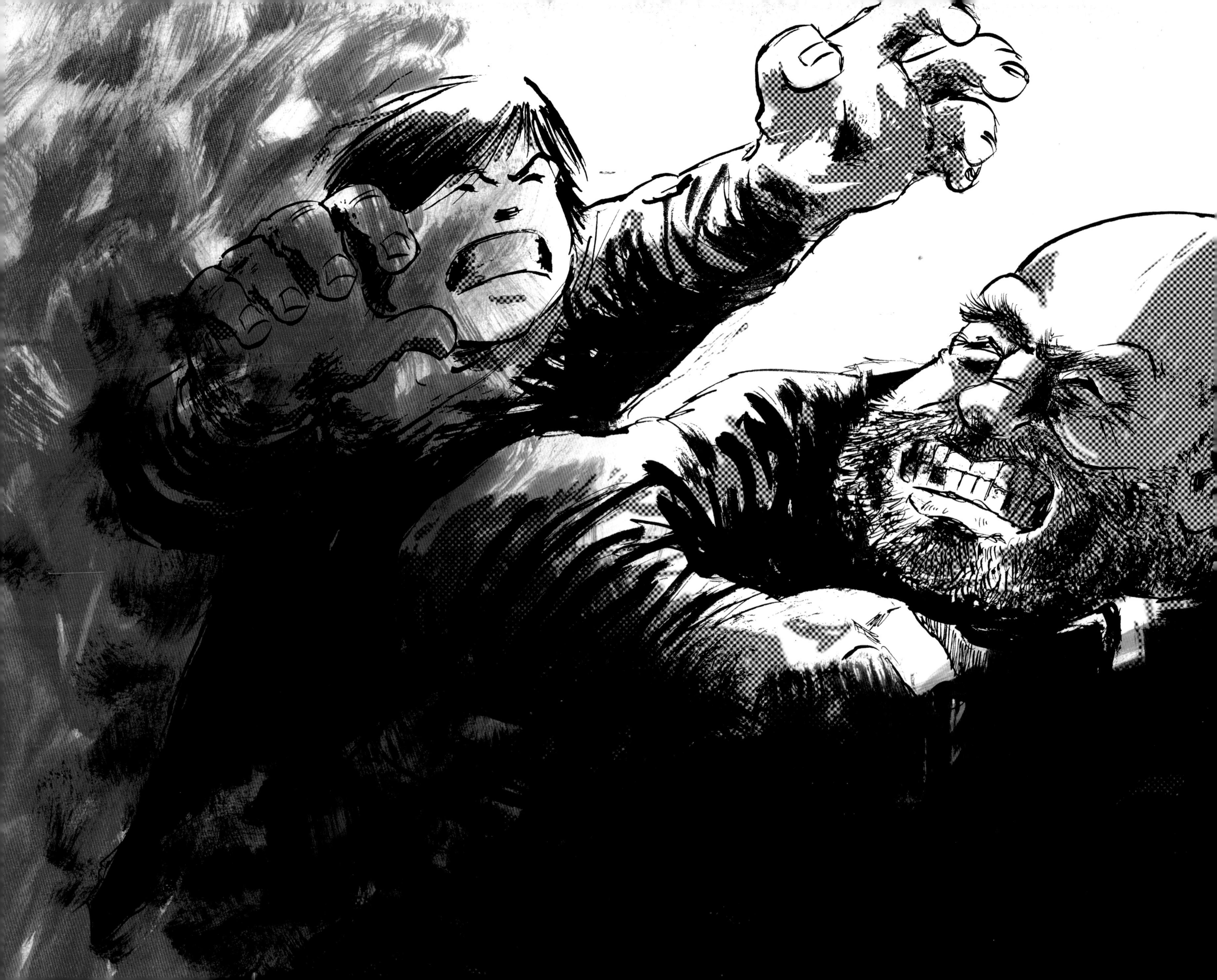

The next thing I remember, I was inside the tavern, and Pop was wiping my face with a cold rag.

"Look at *my* boy, will you?" he was saying. Like he was telling a story to the other men, only real loud. **"Sees his old man on the ground, three big lugs putting the boot in. Does he run away, go find a phone, call the cops, like he's been told to do? Huh! Not *my* lad, disobedient whelp that he is!**

"No, my Sean wades into them like a hell-fired maniac. Three men, there was! Grown men. Yeah, where are all those men now? Still running, is what I'm thinking."

"Probably straight down to the precinct," someone said. "That's where grass goes to grow."

Everybody laughed, but not like at something funny. More like sneering. But not at me. For the first time in my life, not at me.

One of the older guys standing around shouted something. I couldn't understand what he said. Someone else came over and put a big dark sudsy mug in front of me.

"A brave lad who stands up for his Da like you just done, he don't buy his own drinks. Not in *this* house, he don't."

The next thing I remember, it was morning.

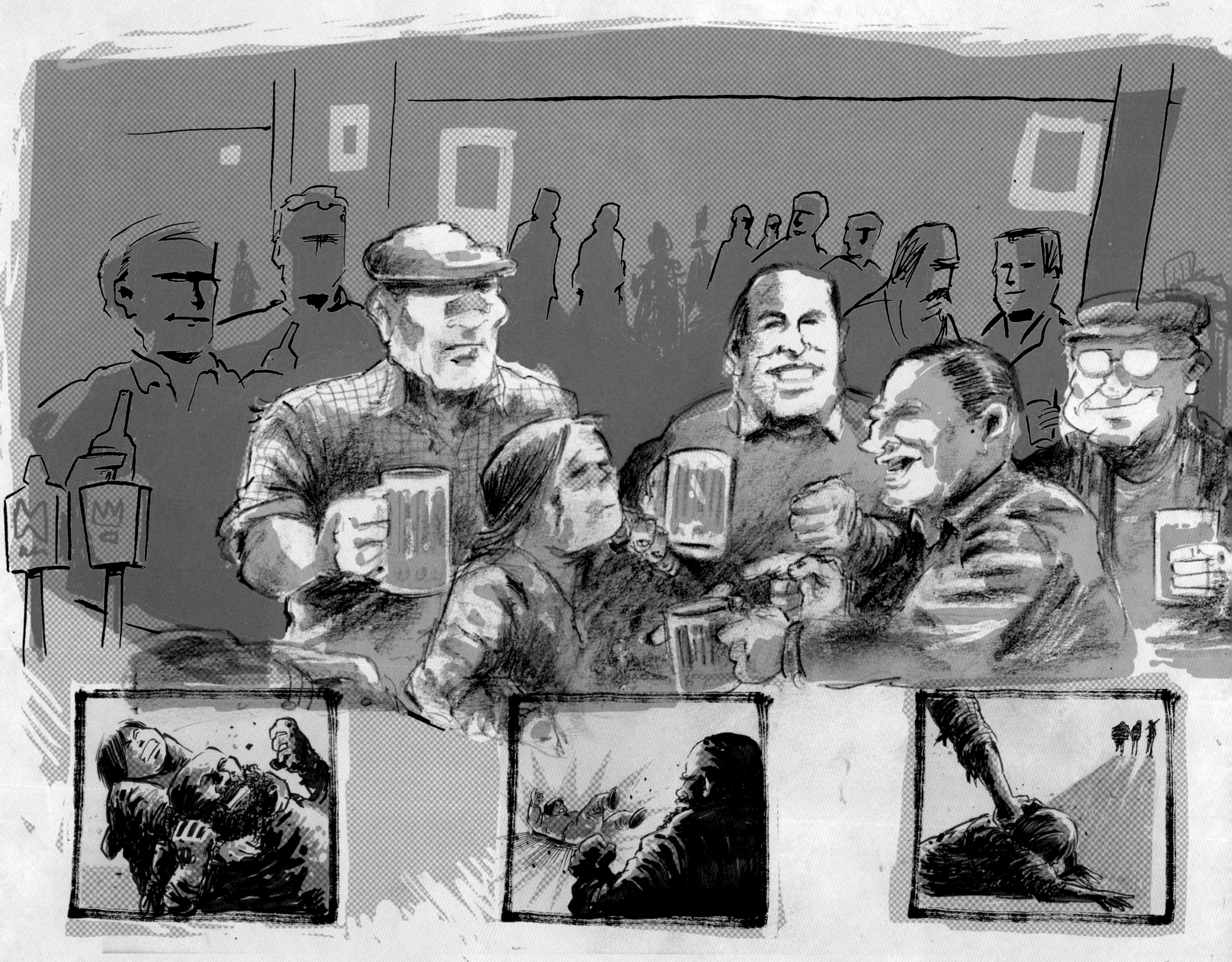

Pop called the school and told them I was sick with the flu. I couldn't make the call myself; I was in the bathroom, throwing up.

It was late afternoon before I could keep any of Pop's special soup down.

"Don't you be developing no taste for that stuff," he warned me. I knew he wasn't talking about the soup.

The next day was Saturday. "I know you hated to miss a day of school, Sean," Pop said. "But it ain't the end of the world. The school even told me they'd be sending all your assignments to your computer. However in God's fancy they do that, I don't know, but the teacher acted like it was no big deal."

"It's true," I said. "I already opened the files."

"So you could, I mean, if you wanted, you could go to school without even being there, right? Graduate and everything?"

"I guess so," I said. I'd never thought about home-schooling before. I knew about it, of course. The School Board has it set up for certain kinds of kids. Handicapped ones, usually. What was the point of sending them to school, anyway? They'd just be outsiders.

"But you never did that?"

"No, sir."

"I could see why you wouldn't want to. Before, I mean. School was probably better than..."

"It was."

"But, you and me, we've been together a long time now, son. You know you're safe here. So how come you never wanted to just stay home and do your work here?"

"I ... I guess I don't know."

"Yeah? Well, *I* know, Sean. You figured there was more to learn than they have in books, right? And you have to go out in the world to find it."

"Maybe. I mean, there *should* be. It's only logical."

"Logical it might be. Thing is, Sean, you always get top marks at school, but you never passed those other courses, did you, now?"

"I don't understand what you're—"

"Come on, Sean. Stop that now; you understand me just perfect. What good is learning about a problem if you can't learn about *solving* the damn thing. Am I right?"

"Yes, sir."

"What you learned, every school you went to, it was always the same. There's different kinds of strength, but the ones who run in groups, they always use their strength on the weak ones, yeah?"

"Yeah," I said. Suddenly, I felt ashamed. Not from being bullied all the time; from never figuring out how to make it stop. I thought about all those sites on the Internet, the ones where they had ... tributes, like ... to kids who went to school with guns and killed a whole bunch of people. I guess I hated the people who were always picking on me, but I never wanted to do anything like that.

"You know what strength is *supposed* to be for, son?"

"How would *I* know?"

"Don't be showing a smart tongue to your old man," he said. He wasn't joking around like he does with me sometimes; his pale blue eyes were like chips of ice. "You listen good, now. God gives people strength for a reason. People who get that gift, they're meant to use it to *protect* the weaker ones, not prey on them.

"Women, like. But not all women. Later on you'll learn that for yourself. But children, they all need protecting, every single one of them.

"And the most precious of all are our *loved* ones, understand? That's why strength is given to us. To *all* of us, in different ways. It's given to us so we can protect our own."

"Like when you came and took me away?"

"*Me?* We're talking about *you* here, Sean. And I didn't take you away; I took you *home*. Remember a couple nights back, you saw your old man getting pounded on. But you didn't use that big brain of yours, did you? Hell, you didn't even *think*, yeah?"

"I ... guess not."

"Were you scared?"

"I ... don't know. I don't *remember* being scared."

"But when some big guy at your school walks up and pokes you in the chest, like *this*," Pop said, "You're scared *then*, right?"

I nodded. Pop's finger felt like a piece of rebar. None of the kids at school, not even the biggest ones, had ever hurt me so much when they jabbed me like that.

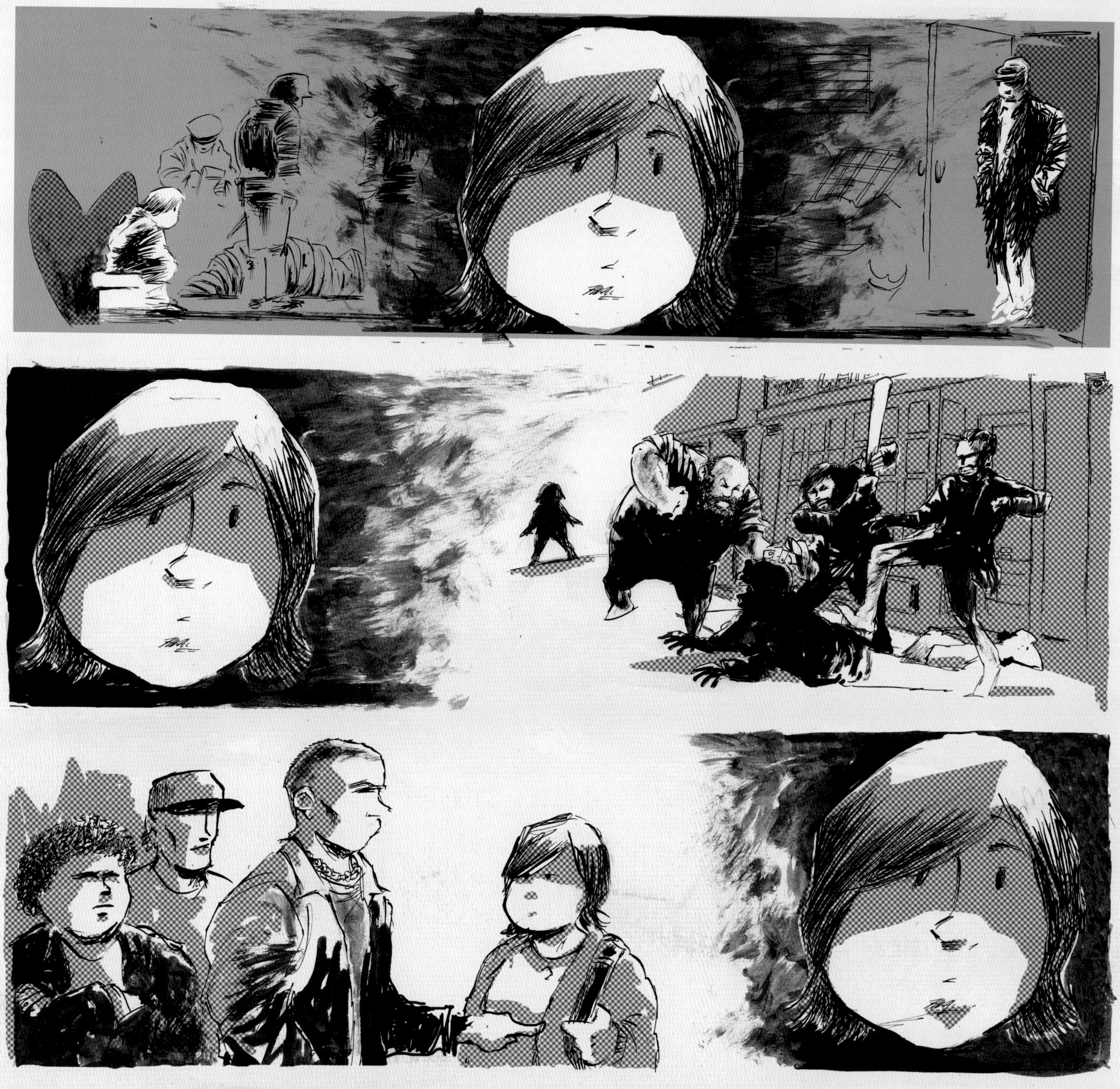

"Yeah, well, that's because you never learned how it works. So I'm going to explain it to you," he said. "It's real simple, son. Some guys, they just like to fight. Known plenty of those kind. Brawlers, they are; it's just the way they're made. Spend as much time in the pubs as I have, you'll not be able to miss them.

"But a bully, he don't want to *fight* you, he wants to *beat* you. A fighter and a bully, they could look like twin brothers, but there's one sure way to always tell them apart."

"How?"

"The more a man wants something, the more he's willing to pay for it. You wanted to stop those men from hurting me, and you didn't care *what* it cost. Isn't that the truth I'm telling you?"

"I didn't even—"

"Right! You, the big brain, you didn't even *think* about it.

"See, thinking's fine when you got choices. Options to consider, like. But when you saw me on the ground, there wasn't none of that. Just one choice. Something that had to be done. And you did it."

"But in school—"

"That ain't *their* choice, Sean. It's yours."

"Pop, I don't understand what you're—"

"How's a man going to know what something's gonna cost him unless he can see a price tag on it? A prizefighter, he knows he's gonna get hit. That's the price, and he's ready to pay it, because he wants the prize he's fighting *for*, see? But a bully, he don't wanna pay any price. That's how you tell them apart."

"I still don't see what you're—"

"You always got to make it cost them something, son. When one of them — even a damn *mob* of them — whales on you, you got to hit back, understand?"

"I don't know how to—"

"Fight? There's only two things you need to know about fighting a bully, boy. One, you don't have to fight fair. Two, there's no way you can lose."

"Can't lose? Me? I'm no—"

"No, no, son. Listen, now. You hurt the other guy, you make *him* feel some pain, then you've *already* won. See, he don't expect to feel *any* pain. He thinks beating on you, that's a free one. Once he finds out it's gonna cost him something, he's going to do his shopping someplace else."

"But they'll still—"

"What, be miserable bullies? Yeah, they will, Sean. And so what? You ain't no damn therapist. Remember that time a bunch of our lads got those drug-peddling swine away from the corner a couple a blocks over? All it took was a few pieces of lumber and a couple of tire irons. And that Shorty, he's still a master of the fire-bottle, too.

"You think that would stop them from selling their dope? Nah. But they don't sell it *here*. See?"

"Yes, sir."

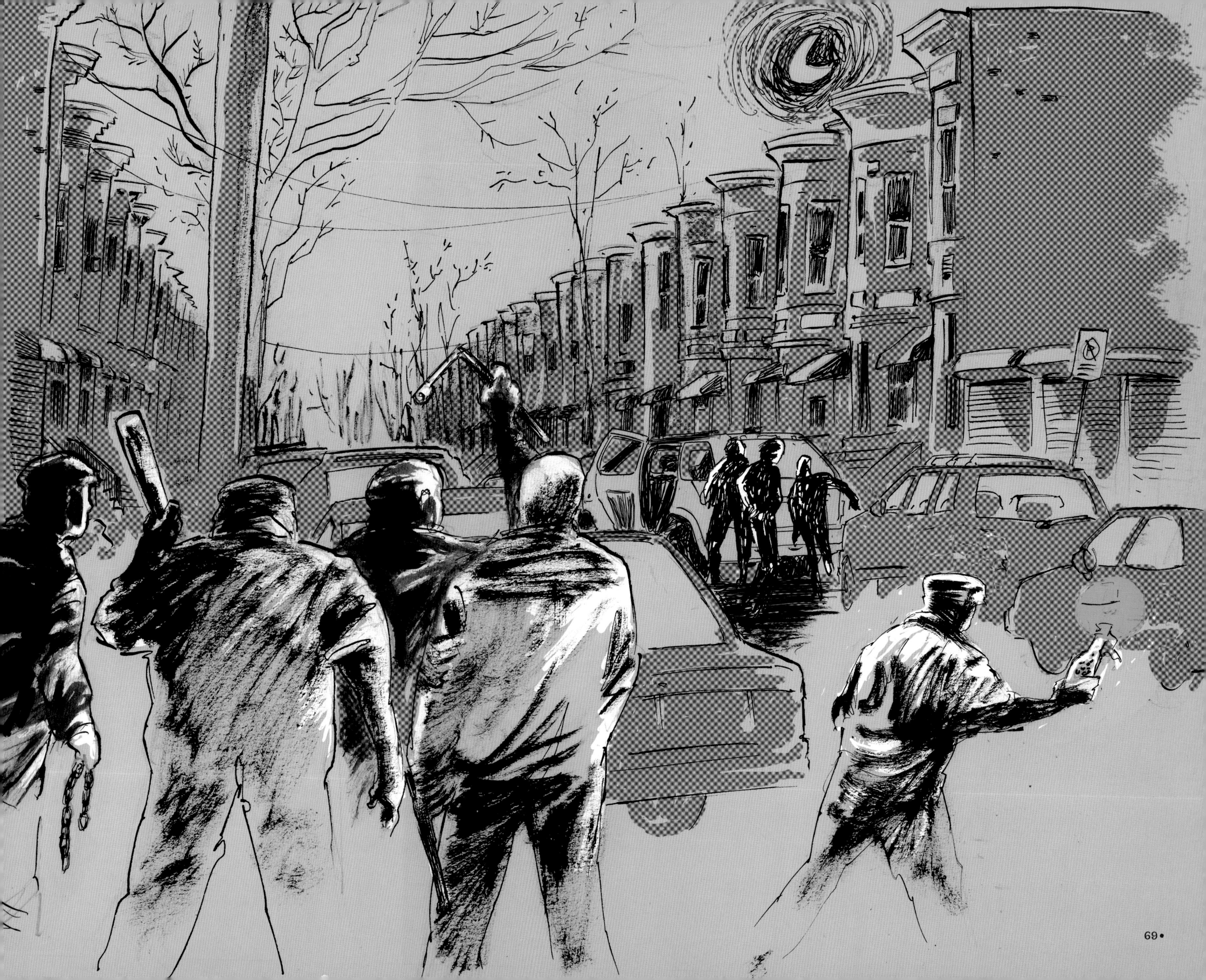

That night, Pop showed me a video. Billy Conn against Joe Louis, for the Heavyweight Championship of the World.

When it was over, he settled back. I knew he was going to tell a tale, so I went into the kitchen and got him a bottle of that dark ale he loves. None of that pale American stuff was allowed in our house.

"Now Billy, he was a light-heavyweight, son. Had no business fighting the big guys. And they didn't come no bigger than Joe. They didn't call him the Brown Bomber for nothing — that man could put you to sleep with either hand.

"But you just saw how our Billy out-boxed him, yeah? He was so fast and smooth that Joe couldn't put a glove on him. By the time they got to the late rounds, Billy was so far ahead that all he had to do was play it smart. Just keep his distance, and he'd be Heavyweight Champion of the World!

"But not our Billy. No, the crazy young fool has to go and try and knock Joe out! And that was all Joe needed, that little opening. One shot, and, *bang!* It was goodnight, nurse."

"So why *didn't* he stay away?"

"Ah, he was an Irishman, boy. Just like you. Only difference between him and you is Billy *knew* what he was. The dumb Mick never even *considered* playing it smart; he just went out there and acted like an Irishman. Same as you did, when you saw your old man getting stomped."

I didn't see it all, then. Not right away.

Sunday, after church, Pop took me to a gym where a lot of different guys hung out that he knew.

The old man Pop had picked to train me looked me over. I could see how dubious he was. I didn't blame him.

"I know he's got the heart, Paddy," he said to Pop. "Your boy, how could that even be a question? But I'm not like some of those Spanish savages; I'm not training no kid just so he can go in there and get himself beat up. Plenty of kids can take it. I know your boy's got that in him. But if that's all he's got, I'm not letting him have a go."

"You think I want my own son turning out like our poor Jerry Quarry, rest his soul?" Pop said. I didn't know what he meant, exactly, but I knew he agreed with what the old man was telling him the minute I saw them shake hands.

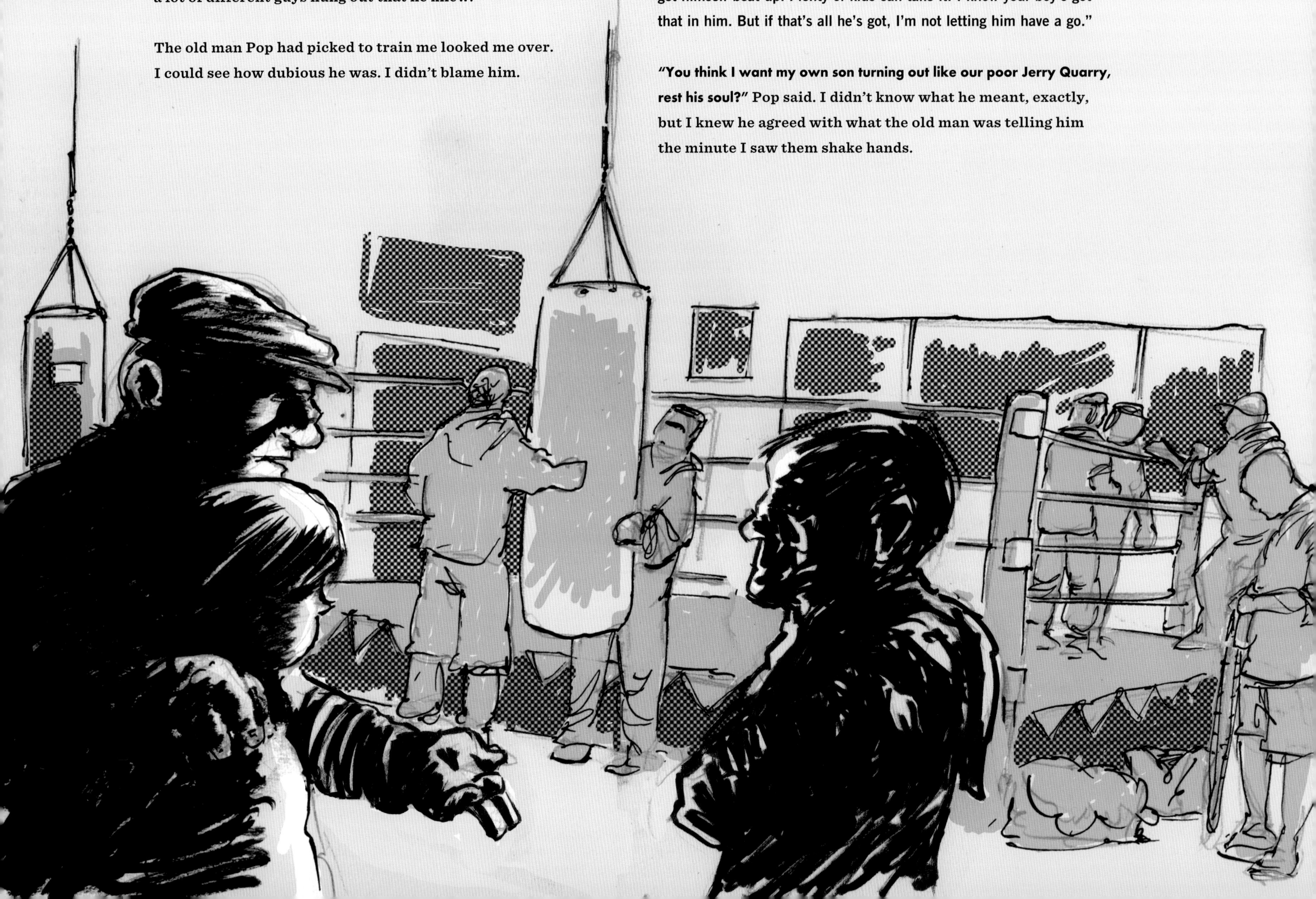

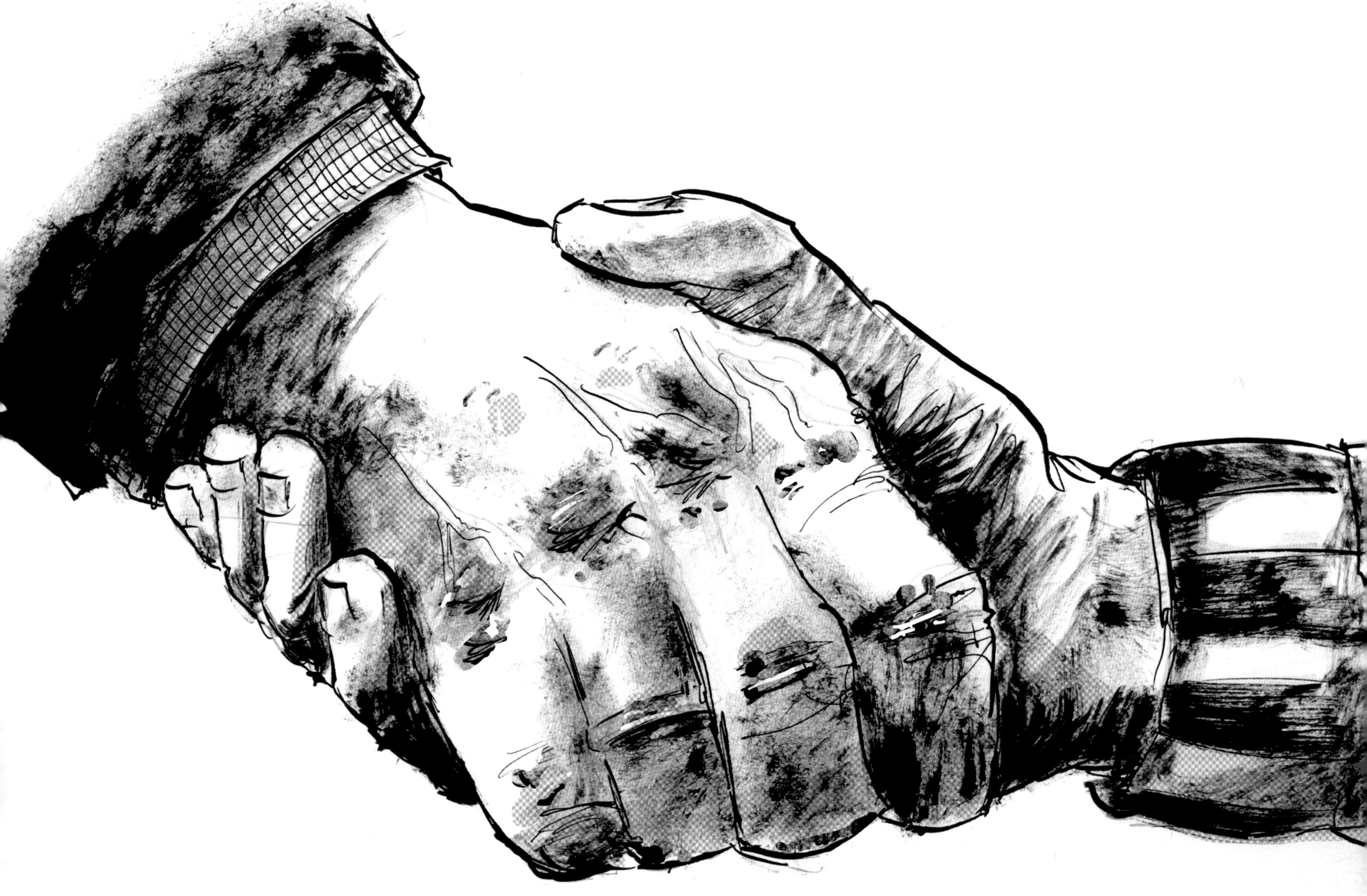

knew I'd have to lose weight. And do roadwork. Work out like
I was back in P.E., cubed. I knew it would take a couple of years
before I could even try out for the Gloves.

I owed it to Pop to put in that time.

But I couldn't wait that long for the rest.

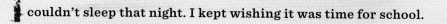

I couldn't sleep that night. I kept wishing it was time for school.

The next morning, when Mario strolled over to my locker with some of the other varsity guys, I didn't wait for whatever he was going to do — I spun around and punched him in the face as hard as I could.

Maybe it was the three rings I had on my right hand that did it. Pop had called them "gougers" when he'd had me try them on. Blood spurted all over Mario's face.

The rest of them went insane. They beat me up so bad that the security guards had to pull them off. They took me to the hospital.

My nose was broken. I couldn't wait for
Pop to see the tape they put all over it.

But, most of all, I couldn't wait for him to
see the bandages they put over my knuckles.
The knuckles on *both* hands.

"Got a few in yourself, didn't you, Seanie?"

"I did, Pop."

"That's my boy. I see they took your rings away, huh?"

"Yes, sir."

"Metal detectors, hah! I knew those lazy mutts would never
pick up something so small inside that knapsack of yours.
And don't be worrying — nobody's gonna bring any
charges. The school already called, and that gang
who jumped you, they're not about to go to court.
Big surprise, that. I can just see them telling a judge
how you jumped on all five of them!

"But they'll be watching you
close now, son. You're not gonna
be able to surprise them twice."

"I know."

"I got this off a fella a long time ago," he said, handing me what looked like a small cylinder of dark wood with a ring at the top. It fit right inside my hand. "Never found any use for it, son. Think you might like to have it?"

wasn't at home when Pop went.
I was a junior in college by then —
the call came in to my dorm.

"It was his heart," the doctor told me, later.
"But that's just the one that won the race. Your father
had serious liver damage, Sean. He only had one lung left
and he had prostate cancer, too ... well-advanced."

"You write whatever you want on
that paper of yours," I told the doctor.
"But you never knew my Pop.
It wasn't his heart that gave out.

It would never be his heart."

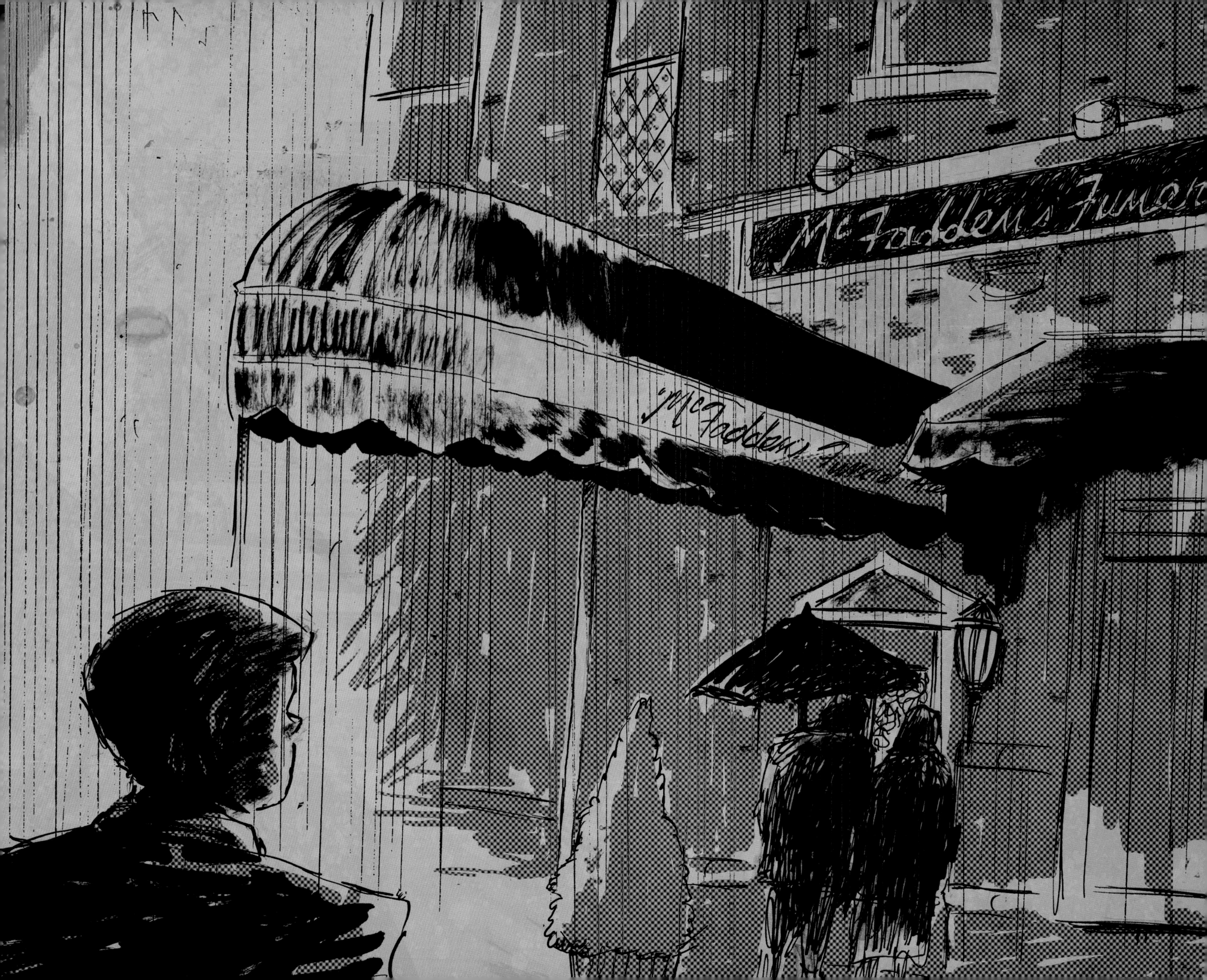
McFadden's
McFadden's

I saw them at the funeral. Even after all those years, I still remembered them. There they stood ... the three men who had been stomping on my Pop outside the tavern that night.

I walked over to them. Slow, so I could keep them all in sight.

"Holy Mother of God! Paddy never told the lad!" one of them said, holding up his hands, palms out, like warding off evil.

I stood there, rooted like a stone tree. Remembering when Pop's pal told me I had no future as a boxer. "You can hit like a freight train, boyo. But you're slow as winter sap. With those pillow gloves and headgear they make you wear in that huge ring, those other kids are gonna just tap you and dance away. If they held these bouts in a phone booth, sure. But..."

Turned out he was right — I'd never gotten past the semis in the Gloves. But I was never stopped, either.

"Sweet Jesus, would you *look* at him?" another one of them said. "He's ready to put us in the ground, right next to his old man. And not sneaking up in the night, with a pistol in his hand. Right here, right now, in front of everyone. Look at his eyes! He's on the kill — Satan himself couldn't stop him.

"That Paddy, God love his scheming mind, he was a pure magician!"

Until that very moment, I thought
I had been the great planner in the
family. But then lightning struck
my stone tree, and the flash drove
out the darkness.

I saw it all, then. When my Pop
saw I needed a heart transplant, he
didn't go to some fancy-ass medical
school to get me one — he gave me
his. Took care of his boy, so his boy
could take care of himself.

Pop, *my* Pop, he hated that movie I'd always been watching in my head. So he re-wrote the script.
And because he wanted it so bad, he paid what it cost.

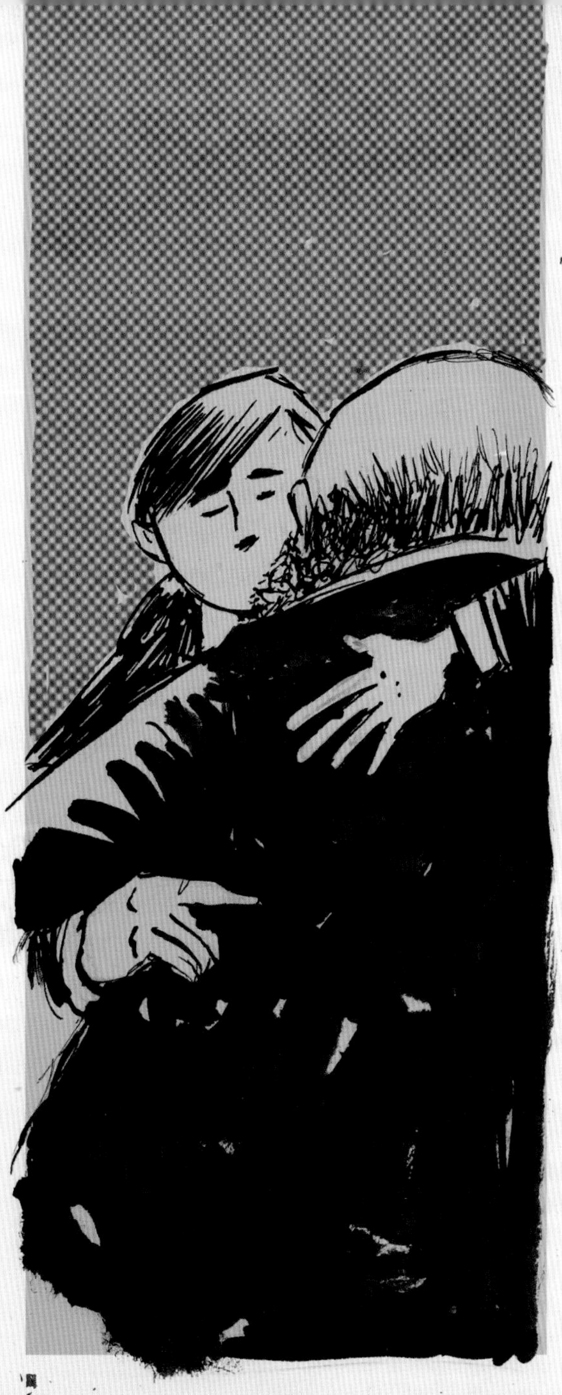

I went over to the three men I thought had been beating up my father outside that tavern so many years ago.

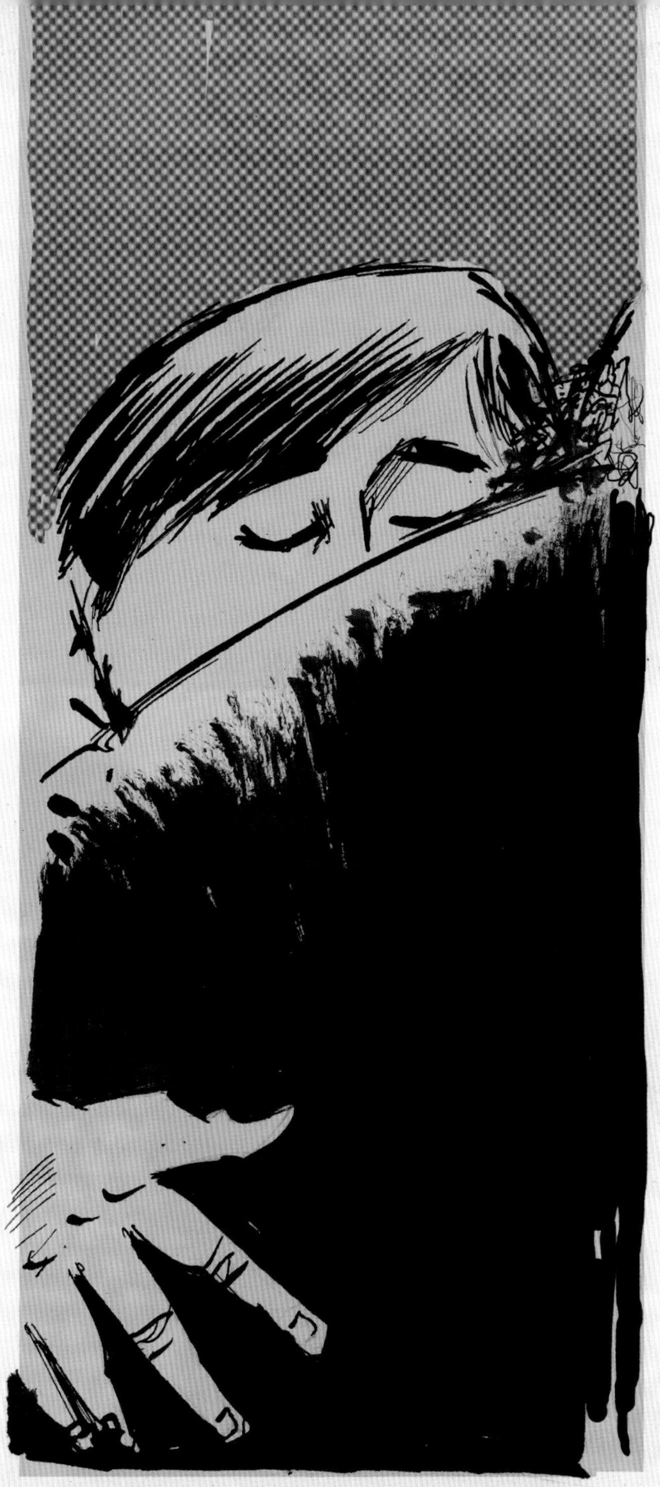

I embraced them all. Kissed their worn cheeks. Swore if they ever needed anything, they had only to ask me.

Me, who knows what a promise means. And what a man's word is worth.

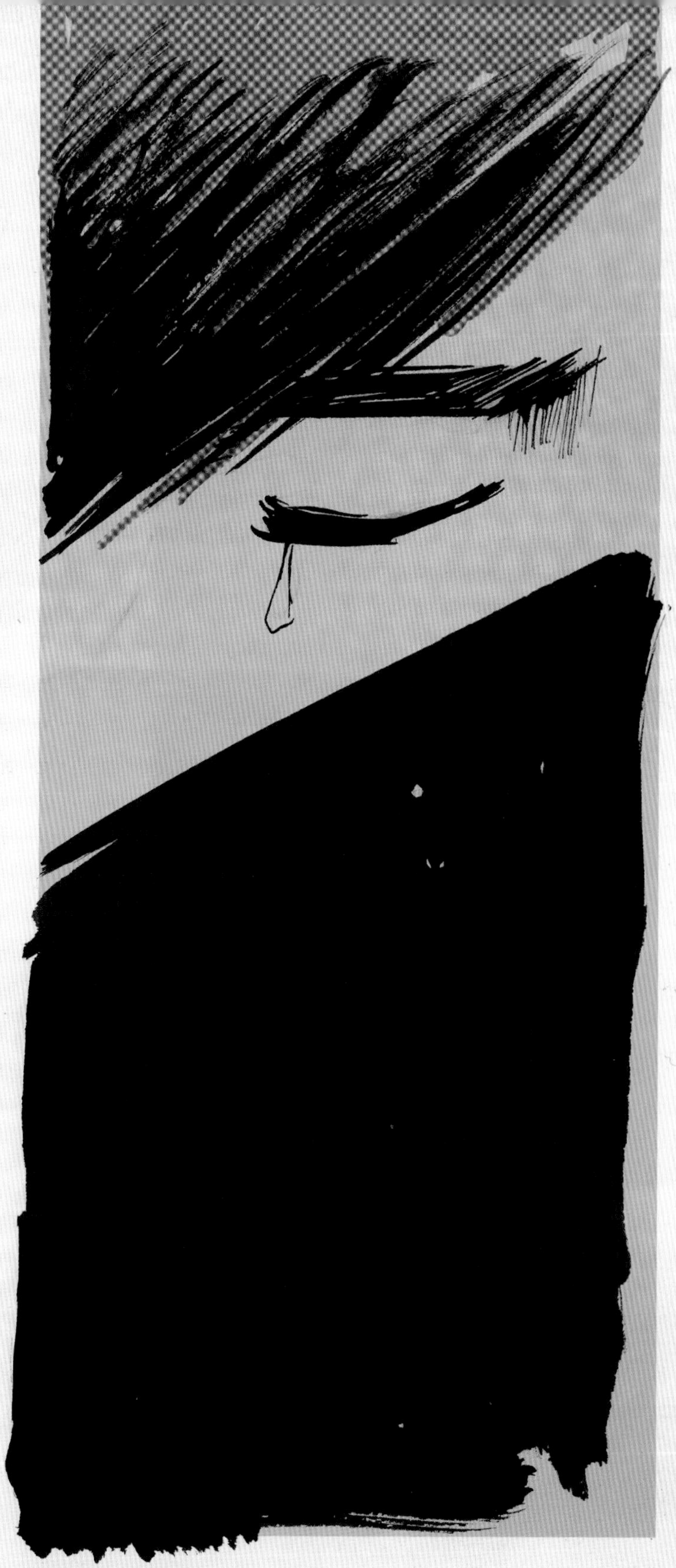

How could I not?

I'm Pop's son, aren't I?

My tears weren't for what I had just lost,
but for what I'd been so blessed to have found.

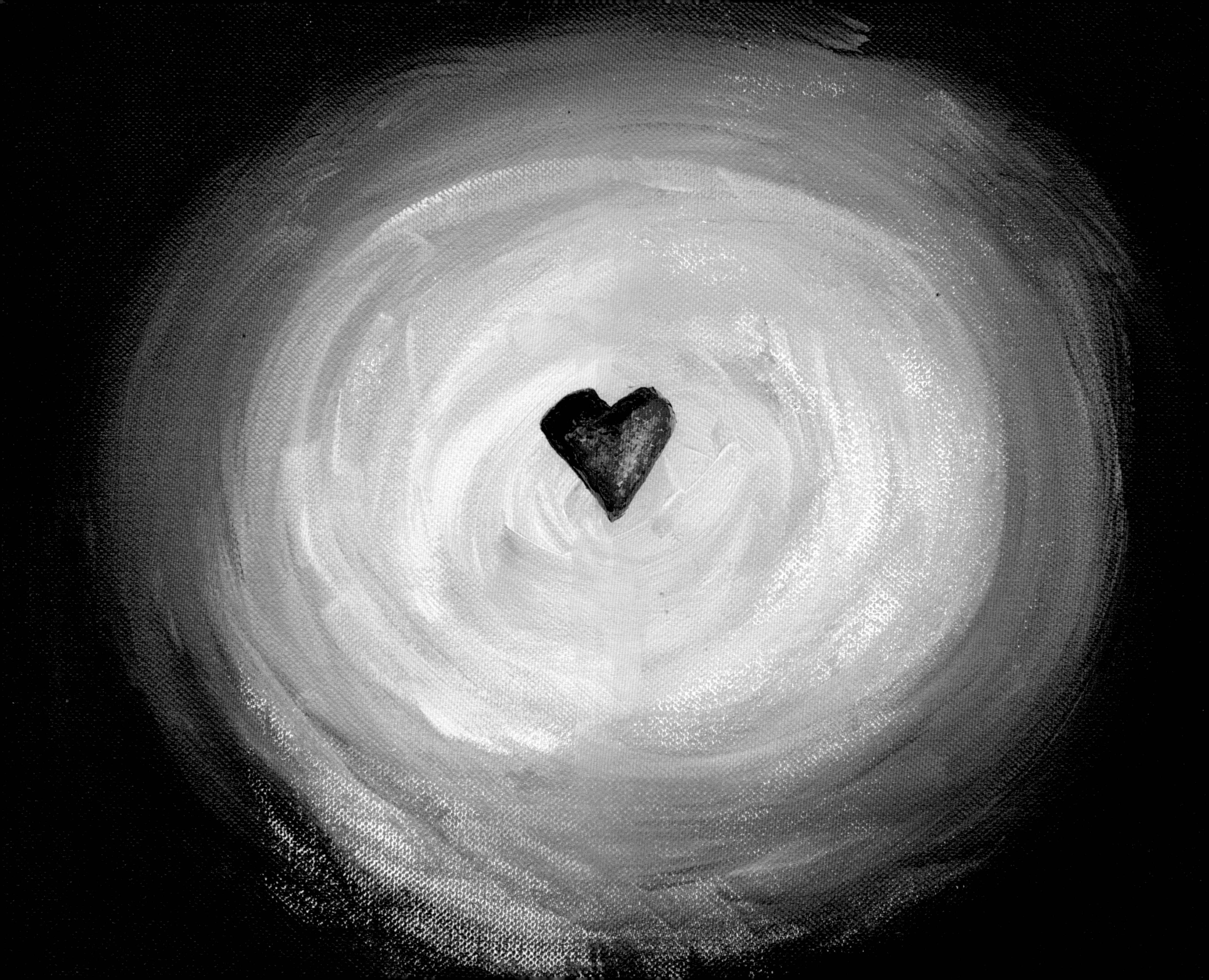

If we expect children to be that resilient, they will never be resilient adults. As adults, they will always seek to remain malleable, thus presenting an easy target to emotional aggressors.

If a victim can decide whom to trust and then act on those decisions, the fallout will repel aggressors attempting to meet their own needs at the expense of others. If a victim can recognize the camouflage of abusers who he is "supposed" to trust and "should" love, if he can recognize the feeling of being engulfed by another's narcissism, then he has the resiliency to emotionally defend himself.

Resiliency acknowledges the world is not an "all or nothing" proposition. Resiliency acknowledges that everyone will have conflict — emotional or physical — throughout his or her life. Resiliency acknowledges there will be a cost. The former victim may lose a "friend," may "cause problems," and may even be perceived as "not nice." These may seem like monumental challenges, but if the victim's own self-diminishment does not eliminate the pain, he must, logically, look outside of himself for the cause.

Doing so lifts the burden the victim assigned himself, but also presents a hard decision: To define one's self, there is a cost. Accepting that cost separates "us" from "them," for "they" — the aggressors — always measure risk and reward, remaining unwilling to fight, but only win.

The courage to withstand those conflicts is necessary. We must be willing to accept conflict, win or lose, to begin creating our own self-definitions. ▮▮▮

RESOURCES

[1]Associated Press. (2009, July 3). Missouri mother says she never should have gone to trial in MySpace hoax case. *Foxnews.com*. Retrieved from http://foxnews.com/story/0,2933,529974,00.html

[2]Segall, L. (2009, July 3). Woman accused of targeting girl, 9, with Craigslist ad. *CNN.com*. Retrieved from http://cnn.com/2009/CRIME/07/03/craigslist.girl/index.html

[3]James, W. (1902). *The varieties of religious experience*. New York, NY: Penguin.

[4]Vachss, A. (1994, August 28). You carry the cure in your own heart. *Parade Magazine*. Retrieved from http://www.vachss.com/av_dispatches/disp_9408_a.html

[5]American Psychiatric Association. (2005). *Diagnostic and statistical manual of mental disorders* (4th ed.). Arlington, VA: American Psychiatric Association.

[6]PDM Task Force. (2006). *Psychodynamic diagnostic manual*. Silver Spring, MD: Alliance of Psychoanalytic Organizations.

[7]Baumeister, R., Bushman, B. J., & Campbell, W. K. (2000). Self-esteem, narcissism, and aggression: Does violence result from low self-esteem or from threatened egotism? *Current Directions in Psychological Science, 9*. (1).

[8]Wilson, C., & Piman, P. (1961). *The encyclopaedia of murder*. New York, London and Sydney: Pan Books.

[9]Wolfe, T. (2009, September 24). $1 million settlement reached in 2005 shooting near Sandy. *The Oregonian*. Retrieved from http://www.oregonlive.com/clackamascounty/index.ssf/2009/07/sandy_settles_kaady_case

[10]Twenge, J. M., & Campbell, W. K. (2009). *The narcissism epidemic: Living in the age of entitlement*. New York, NY: Free Press.

[11]Perry, B. D. (2002). Childhood experience and the expression of genetic potential: What childhood neglect tells us about nature and nurture. *Brain and Mind, 3*. 79-100.

[12]Decety, J., Michalska, K. J., Akitsuki, Y., & Lahey, B. B. (2008). Atypical empathetic responses in adolescents with aggressive conduct disorder: A functional MRI investigation. *Biological Psychology*. Doi:10.1016/j.biopsycho.2008.09.004

[13]Simmons, R. (2002). *Odd girl out: The hidden culture of aggression in girls*. New York, NY: Harcourt.

[14]Perry, B. D. (1997). Incubated in terror: Neurodevelopmental factors in the 'cycle of violence.' In J. Osofsky (Ed.), *Children, youth, and violence*. New York, NY: Guilford Press.

[15]Stettbacher, J. K. (1993). *Making sense of suffering: The healing confrontation with your own past*. (Trans., S. Worral), New York, NY: Meridian.

[16]Gaddis, T. E., & Long, J. O. (2002). *Panzram: A journal of murder*. Los Angeles, CA: Amok.

[17]Fox News Network. (2007, April 19). Virginia Tech gunman mailed video rant before murderous rampage; Court records show killer was ruled a danger in 2005. *Foxnews.com*. Retrieved from http://foxnews.com/story/0,2933,266683,00.html. *Also see* Potter, N., Schoetz, D., Esposito, R., & Thomas, P. (2007, April 17). Killer's note: 'You caused me to do this.' *ABCnews.com*. Retrieved from http://abcnews.go.com/US/story?id=3048108&page=1.html

[18]Cullen, D. (2009). *Columbine*. New York, NY: Hachette Book Group.

[19]Freyd, J. J. (1996). *Betrayal trauma*. Cambridge, MA: Harvard.

[20]Miller, A. (1981). *The drama of the gifted child*. (Trans., R. Ward), New York, NY: Basic Books.

[21]Winnicott, D. W. (1986). *Home is where we start from*. New York, NY: W.W. Norton.